Contact Information

Published by:

Currex Investment Services Inc.
Web site: http://www.forexmentor.com
Email: info@forexmentor.com
Updates: http://www.forexmentor.com/updates

Copyright © 2003-2008 Currex Investment Services Inc., All rights reserved.
Revision Date: April, 2008

Legal Notices & Disclaimer

Peter Bain's Currency Trading system and trading methodologies referenced in this product are analytical tools only, and are not intended to replace individual research or licensed investment advice. Unique experiences and past performances do not guarantee future results. Testimonials are not representative of all clients. Trading currencies involves substantial risk, and there is always the potential for significant loss. Your trading results may vary. No representation is being made that these products, and any associated advice or training, methods, strategies, tips will guarantee profits, or not result in losses from trading. Neither the products, any explanation or demonstration of their operation, nor any training held in conjunction therewith, including, without limitation, through online or offline content, in conjunction with our advertising and promotional campaigns, during our live seminars or otherwise, should be construed as providing a trade recommendation or the giving of investment advice. The purchase, sale or advice regarding a currency can only be performed by a licensed Broker/Dealer. Neither Currex Investment Services, nor any of its affiliates or associates involved in the production and maintenance of these products or website, is a registered Broker/Dealer or Investment Advisor in any Province, State or Federally-sanctioned jurisdiction. All purchasers of products referenced at this site are encouraged to consult with a licensed representative of their choice regarding a particular trade or trading strategy.

WELCOME

Congratulations on your investment in Forexmentor!

By becoming a Forexmentor member, you have taken an important first step towards becoming a successful trader in the Forex market. Our team of mentors is ready to support and serve you on this exciting journey.

As a valued Forexmentor member, you are entitled to many additional educational resources – all designed and developed with one purpose in mind: *To empower you as a currency trader.*

Please take advantage of these valuable resources by logging onto the members' area (www.forexmentor.com/login) to gain access to the following:

1) Daily AM Review Market Analysis with Peter Bain
2) Daily Pivot Data for all major currency pairs
3) Online Training Video Library
4) Searchable Database & Frequently Asked Questions
5) Member Discussion Forum
6) Member Contributions/File Library
7) Currency Trading Tips & Updates
8) Guest Speakers

…and many other resources.

We'd like to hear from you! If you require assistance from our team, please contact us via email at *info@forexmentor.com*. If you have suggestions on how we can improve your learning experience, please write to us. Finally, we love to hear success stories from our members. These stories really make our day! They are also encouraging to those who may be struggling with their trading.

Our ultimate goal at Forexmentor is to provide the necessary tools to make this a successful journey for you.

From Peter & the Entire Forexmentor Team

How to Proceed Through This Course

1. Start by watching the *Currency Trading Video Seminar DVDs* (set of 2)

2. Go through the *Currency Trading Video Course* manual

3. Watch the accompanying video tutorials referenced throughout the manual on the *Currency Trading Video CDs* (12 CDs)

4. Watch daily *AM Reviews* (Tuesday – Friday)

    Go through the archives of the AM Reviews or use the AM Review Online Search Engine to locate specific subjects discussed by Peter in his AM Review videos.

    AM Review Archive (September 2003 to present)
    AM Review Online Search Engine (November 2005 to present)

5. Go through the *Video Tutorial Library* (150+ hours of online streaming video tutorials) for additional information helpful for mastering the basics.

6. Review *Forex Trading Tips*

Go to www.forexmentor.com/protect/getting-started-steps.html for additional information and links to resources discussed above.

Table of Contents

Part I Basic Technical Analysis Tools

How Price Moves 21
Support and Resistance 25
Price Patterns 33
Pivot Points 55
Candlesticks 77
Trendlines 97
MACD 115
Stochastics 129
Price Projections 135
Time of Day 143
Commitment of Traders (COT) 151
Top Down Trading 163
Risk Management 179
Homework - Do It or Get Schooled 181
Patience 185
What is Forex and What is a Pip? 191
What Moves the Forex Market 197
Your Trading Plan 203
Choosing a Forex Broker 207
How to Place a Trade 211
How to Set Up Your Charts 219
How to Treat Demo Trading 233
What You Should Consider Before Trading REAL Money 235
Taking Care of the Trader 237
Final Comments 243
Glossary 245
Index 253

Video CD Index

Part I Basic Technical Analysis Tools

CD DISK 1: Price Patterns

1-2-3 Tops
1.1. Identifying 1-2-3 Tops (01:08)
1.2. 1-2-3 Top Example (00:45)

1-2-3 Bottoms
1.3. Identifying 1-2-3 Bottoms (02:23)
1.4. What Does a 1-2-3 Bottom Look Like (00:42)
1.5. 1-2-3 Bottom Example (00:35)
1.6. 1-2-3 Bottom Trading Example 1 (02:02)
1.7. 1-2-3 Bottom Trading Example 2 (02:13)

Double Tops
1.8. Double Top Example (00:35)

Double Bottoms
1.9. Double Bottom Example (00:42)

Head and Shoulders
1.10. Head and Shoulders Example 1 (02:26)
1.11. Head and Shoulders Example 2 (00:39)
1.12. Head and Shoulders Example 3 (00:42)
1.13. Head and Shoulders Examples (00:19)
1.14. How to Trade a Head and Shoulders (00:27)

Inverted Head and Shoulders
1.15. Inverted Head and Shoulders Example (01:32)

Bull Flags
1.16. Bull Flag Example 1 (00:15)
1.17. Bull Flag Example 2 (00:40)
1.18. Bull Flag in an Uptrend (01:31)

Bear Flags
1.19. Bear Flag Example 1 (00:23)
1.20. Bear Flag Example 2 (00:23)
1.21. Bear Flag in a Downtrend (01:27)
1.22. How to Plot a Flag (00:39)

Triangles in an Uptrend
1.23. Triangle Example 1 (00:28)
1.24. Triangle Example 2 (01:03)
1.25. Triangle Example 3 (01:29)

1.26. Triangle Trading Example (00:39)

Triangles in a Downtrend
1.27. Triangle Example 1 (00:29)
1.28. Triangle Example 2 (00:34)
1.29. Triangle Example 3 (01:48)
1.30. Triangle Example 4 (02:22)
1.31. Triangle Example 5 (00:32)
1.32. Triangle Example 6 (01:19)
1.33. Triangle Trading Example (01:00)
1.34. How to Draw Triangles (01:00)

CD DISK 2

2. Pivot Points
Pivot Points
2.1. Pivot Points Origin (00:43)
2.2. Pivot Points Overview 1 (03:44)
2.3. Pivot Points Overview 2 (02:47)
2.4. Pivot Points Overview 3 (02:03)
2.5. Marking Pivot Points on Charts (04:30)

How to Calculate the Pivots
2.6. Calculating Pivot Points Overview 1 (02:42)
2.7. Calculating Pivot Points Overview 2 (04:51)
2.8. Posting of Pivot Points (00:24)
2.9. Projected Range and Actual Range (01:33)
2.10. Recalculating Pivot Points 1 (02:55)
2.11. Recalculating Pivot Points 2 (01:35)
2.12. Calculating Daily Pivot Points 1 (00:48)
2.13. Calculating Daily Pivot Points 2 (11:10)
2.14. Calculating Pivots Points Using the Daily Chart (01:39)
2.15. Calculating Weekly Pivot Points 1 (00:58)
2.16. Calculating Weekly Pivot Points 2 (08:33)
2.17. Calculating Monthly and Yearly Pivot Points (00:19)
2.18. Calculating Monday Pivot Points 1 (01:16)
2.19. Calculating Monday Pivot Points 2 (05:24)
2.20. Calculating Holiday Pivot Points (06:44)

How to Use the Pivot Points
2.21. Pivot Points and Bias 1 (01:43)
2.22. Pivot Points and Bias 2 (03:25)
2.23. Pivot Points and Bias 3 (01:36)
2.24. Pivots Points Trading Example 1 (02:36)
2.25. Pivots Points Trading Example 2 (00:48)
2.26. Trading on Pivot Points Retest (02:51)

M1/M3, M2/M4 Paradigm
2.27. M1/M3, M2/M4 Paradigm Explained 1 (04:45)

2.28. M1/M3, M2/M4 Paradigm Explained 2 (01:02)
2.29. M1/M3, M2/M4 Paradigm Clarified 1 (00:59)
2.30. M1/M3, M2/M4 Paradigm Clarified 2 (01:15)
2.31. M1/M3, M2/M4 Paradigm Clarified 3 (01:38)
2.32. M2/M4 Example (01:44)

CD DISK 3: Candlesticks

Components of a Candlestick
3.1. Constructing Candlesticks (00:30)

Spinning Tops
3.2. A Lesson in Spinning Tops (00:28)
3.3. Spinning Top Example (00:31)

The Hammer
3.4. A Lesson in Hammers (01:57)
3.5. Hammer Example 1 (00:30)
3.6. Hammer Example 2 (00:21)
3.7. Hammer Application in Trading (02:38)
3.8. Hammers Only Work at End of Run (01:17)
3.9. Inverted Hammer Significance in a Downtrend (01:38)

Railroad Tracks
3.10. A Lesson in Railroad Tracks 1 (00:45)
3.11. A Lesson in Railroad Tracks 2 (04:43)
3.12. Railroad Tracks Example 1 (00:37)
3.13. Railroad Tracks Example 2 (00:27)
3.14. Railroad Tracks Example 3 (00:36)
3.15. Railroad Tracks Example 4 (00:12)
3.16. Railroad Tracks Example 5 (00:57)
3.17. Railroad Tracks Example 6 (01:09)
3.18. Railroad Tracks Trading Example (01:53)
3.19. Railroad Tracks Size (01:05)
3.20. Railroad Tracks Not Correctly Formed (01:02)

CD DISK 4: Trendlines

Common Sense Trendlines
4.1. Common Sense Trendlines Example 1 (03:40)
4.2. Common Sense Trendlines Example 2 (05:52)
4.3. Common Sense Trendlines Trading Example 1 (02:24)
4.4. Common Sense Trendlines Trading Example 2 (01:54)

Tom DeMark Trendlines
4.5. Tom DeMark Dynamic Trendlines (01:06)

Swing Points
4.6. Determining Swing Points 1 (02:11)

4.7. Determining Swing Points 2 (01:44)
4.8. Finding Swing Points (03:11)

TD Supply Lines
4.9. Constructing TD Supply Lines (01:24)

TD Demand Lines
4.10. Constructing TD Demand Lines (01:40)

TD Trendlines Examples
4.11. TD Trendlines Example 1 (01:18)
4.12. TD Trendlines Example 2 (05:44)
4.13. TD Trendlines Example 3 (06:10)
4.14. TD Trendlines Example 4 (01:21)
4.15. TD Trendlines Example 5 (02:07)
4.16. TD Trendlines Example 6 (00:46)
4.17. TD Trendlines Example 7 (00:34)
4.18. TD Trendlines Example 8 (01:11)
4.19. TD Trendlines Example 9 (01:04)
4.20. TD Trendlines Example 10 (07:48)
4.21. TD Trendlines Example 11 (01:35)
4.22. TD Trendlines Drawing Example 1 (06:41)
4.23. TD Trendlines Drawing Example 2 (06:17)
4.24. TD Trendlines Drawing Example 3 (15:51)
4.25. TD Trendlines Drawing Example 4 (16:03)
4.26. TD Trendlines Drawing Example 5 (17:38)
4.27. TD Trendlines Drawing Example 6 (10:17)
4.28. TD Trendlines Drawing Example 7 (10:47)
4.29. TD Trendlines Drawing Example 8 (17:22)
4.30. TD Trendlines Drawing Example 9 (07:34)
4.31. TD Trendlines Drawing Example 10 (07:39)

CD DISK 5: MACD

MACD Indicator
5.1. MACD Histogram Examples (06:19)
5.2. MACD Neutral Line (01:19)

MACD Neutralization and Divergence
5.3. How Reliable is Divergence (00:33)

MACD Divergence
5.4. MACD Divergence Examples (10:02)
5.5. MACD Negative Divergence Example 1 (02:22)
5.6. MACD Negative Divergence Example 2 (04:44)
5.7. MACD Negative Divergence Example 3 (00:47)
5.8. MACD Negative Divergence Example 4 (03:22)
5.9. MACD Negative Divergence Example 5 (01:58)
5.10. MACD Negative Divergence Example 6 (02:25)

5.11. MACD Negative Divergence Example 7 (02:53)
5.12. MACD Negative Divergence Example 8 (00:53)
5.13. MACD Positive Divergence Example 1 (01:13)
5.14. MACD Positive Divergence Example 2 (00:24)
5.15. MACD Positive Divergence Example 3 (00:43)
5.16. MACD Positive Divergence Example 4 (01:53)
5.17. Importance of Divergence in Higher Timeframes (00:32)

MACD Neutralization
5.18. MACD Neutralization Explained 1 (15:05)
5.19. MACD Neutralization Explained 2 (05:52)
5.20. MACD Neutralization Explained 3 (03:56)
5.21. MACD Neutralization Explained 4 (05:14)
5.22. MACD Neutralization or Divergence (01:45)
5.23. MACD Neutralization Example 1 (01:36)
5.24. MACD Neutralization Example 2 (01:33)
5.25. MACD Neutralization Example 3 (01:26)
5.26. MACD Neutralization Example 4 (01:19)
5.27. MACD Neutralization Example 5 (03:21)

CD DISK 6

Stochastics Indicator
6.1. Trading With Stochastics (07:01)
6.2. Using Stochastics (02:05)
6.3. Buying the Dips in an Uptrend with Stochastics (00:33)
6.4. Trading into a Trend Using Stochastics and MACD (03:06)

Average Daily Range Price Projections
7.1. Determining the Average Daily Range (01:54)
7.2. Average Daily Range Explained (02:26)
7.3. Average Daily Range 24 Hours (00:25)
7.4. Average Daily Range Data 1 (00:35)
7.5. Average Daily Range Data 2 (00:48)
7.6. Average Daily Range for Various Currency Pairs (00:35)
7.7. Average Daily Range Analysis (01:32)
7.8. Average Daily Range Clarified (03:08)
7.9. Average Daily Range Varies Day to Day (01:17)
7.10. Average Daily Range for EURUSD (01:59)

Triangle Price Projections
7.11. Triangle Price Projection 1 (01:13)
7.12. Triangle Price Projection 2 (01:51)
7.13. Triangle Price Projection 3 (02:01)

Head and Shoulders Price Projections
7.14. Head and Shoulders Price Projection 1 (02:51)
7.15. Head and Shoulders Price Projection 2 (05:11)
7.16. Inverted Head and Shoulders Price Projection (05:42)

Time of Day
8.1. Forex Hours of Operation by Location 1 (01:56)
8.2. Forex Hours of Operation by Location 2 (01:56)
8.3. Times of the Day Chart (02:03)
8.4. GMT Times of the Markets (00:46)
8.5. Time and Date Link (00:43)
8.6. World Market Hours Link (00:55)
8.7. Time Zone Conversion (00:27)
8.8. Daylight Savings (01:07)

Clocks
8.9. A Members FX Market Time Program (00:54)
8.10. SymmTime Clock (00:17)
8.11. ZoneTick Clock (00:29)
8.12. Clock Software (00:29)
8.13. Clocks, Clocks, and More Clocks (02:47)

Specific Times of Day
8.14. Times of the Day to Watch Out For (00:29)
8.15. Important Trading Times (01:11)
8.16. Reversal at the London Open (00:31)
8.17. Pay Attention to Certain Times of Day (00:44)
8.18. Grabbing 20 Pips at the London Close (00:32)
8.19. A Caution on Open and Close Times 1 (01:52)
8.20. A Caution on Open and Close Times 2 (03:05)

Trading Sessions
8.21. Forex Daily Trading Activity (00:37)
8.22. Non-London Trading Hours (01:01)
8.23. Asian Hour Trading (00:38)
8.24. What Time to Start Trading (01:26)

CD DISK 7: Commitment of Traders (COT)

9.1. COT Website Introduction (02:09)
9.2. Main Report Page Explanation (08:52)
9.3. Euro FX Report Introduction (01:48)
9.4. Finding the Euro FX Report at the CFTC Website (08:49)
9.5. Date and Commercial Contracts Explanation (22:31)
9.6. Speculator Contracts Explanation (11:55)
9.7. Small Trader Explanation (17:09)
9.8. Open Interest and Future Price Explanation (05:41)

CD DISK 8: Commitment of Traders (COT), Part II

9.9. Graph COT Index and Net Position Explanation (29:16)
9.10. Graph COT Index and Net Position Application (18:04)
9.11. Graph COT, Spec, Small Index/Price Explanation (17:25)
9.12. Graph COT, Spec, Small Index/Price Application (13:17)
9.13. How COT Works 1 (12:50)
9.14. How COT Works 2 (07:21)
9.15. How COT Works 3 (09:02)
9.16. When to Enter (01:14)
9.17. Be Patient with COT (01:31)
9.18. Independent Research on COT (00:52)

COT Examples
9.19. Australian Dollar Example 1 (02:01)
9.20. Australian Dollar Example 2 (05:44)
9.21. Australian Dollar Example 3 (02:36)
9.22. Australian Dollar Example 4 (05:18)
9.23. Australian Dollar Example Brag Time (03:01)

Part II: Putting the Tools to Work

CD DISK 9

Top Down Trading
10.1. Top Down Trading 1 (05:29)
10.2. Top Down Trading 2 (01:16)
10.3. Top Down Trading Example 1 (21:55)
10.4. Top Down Trading Example 2 (10:01)
10.5. Top Down Trading and Timeframes (00:53)
10.6. Top Down Analysis in Short Term Trading (01:27)
10.7. Reading the Charts Top Down (02:58)

Confluence of Events
10.8. The 21 Pieces of the Confluence Puzzle (01:00)
10.9. Confluence of Events Reminder (01:44)
10.10. The Perfect Peter Bain Trade 1 (02:43)
10.11. The Perfect Peter Bain Trade 2 (06:41)
10.12. Confluence of Indicators (02:08)
10.13. Understanding Confluence (01:47)
10.14. Using Confluence Examples (05:01)
10.15. Detecting Confluence Using Side by Side Charts (03:16)

CD DISK 10

Historical Trading Examples
10.16. February 17, 2005 (15:24)
10.17. February 23, 2005 (08:28)

10.18. February 24, 2005 (08:55)
10.19. March 1, 2005 (05:27)
10.20. March 2, 2005 (14:37)
10.21. March 3, 2005 (07:40)
10.22. March 4, 2005 (07:03)
10.23. March 10, 2005 (05:20)
10.24. March 24, 2005 (10:58)
10.25. March 25, 2005 (12:20)
10.26. March 29, 2005 (06:26)
10.27. March 31, 2005 (07:08)
10.28. April 7, 2005 (11:30)
10.29. April 28, 2005 (12:31)
10.30. May 3, 2005 (10:13)
10.31. May 4, 2005 (03:02)
10.32. May 5, 2005 (16:03)
10.33. May 6, 2005 (05:13)
10.34. May 10, 2005 (08:16)
10.35. May 11, 2005 (09:51)
10.36. May 12, 2005 (13:18)
10.37. May 13, 2005 (10:24)

CD DISK 11

Risk Management
11.1. Money Management Considerations (02:19)

Homework
12.1. Keep a Log (01:18)
12.2. Write Things Down (00:30)
12.3. The Importance of Taking Notes (04:10)
12.4. Setting Up a Trading Log (01:20)
12.5. Keeping a Trading Journal (01:33)
12.6. Printing AM Review Slides (02:50)
12.7. Crosschecking Your Work (01:44)

13. Patience
Patience
13.1. Patience to Wait for Opportunities (01:35)
13.2. It All Takes Time (01:12)
13.3. Patience Folks (02:29)
13.4. Impatience Can Kill You (00:26)
13.5. Patience (03:17)

Part III: Things You Need to Know About the Forex

CD DISK 12

14. What is Forex and What is a Pip
The Currency Pairs
14.1. The Mechanics of the Trading Pairs (00:33)
14.2. Trading Pairs Terminology (00:54)
14.3. Pip Spreads (03:30)
14.4. The Four Major Pairs (01:25)
14.5. Most Active Pairs (00:52)
14.6. Which Pair Should I Specialize In (00:37)

Pips
14.7. What is a Pip (00:34)
14.8. Pip Values (00:37)
14.9. Pip Values Updated (01:09)

15. What Moves the Forex Market
News
15.1. Risky Trading the News (01:11)
15.2. The Effect of News (01:56)
15.3. News Source Links (00:38)
15.4. Non-Farm Payroll News (01:02)
15.5. Start of the Iraq War (01:40)
15.6. Daily Diary of Upcoming Events (00:35)
15.7. News Calendar Link (00:29)
15.8. Bloomberg as a News Resource (00:14)
15.9. Fundamental News Analysis (01:17)
15.10. News Trumping the Technicals (00:41)

16. Your Trading Plan
Trading Plan
16.1. Develop Your Own Trading Style (01:01)

17. Choosing a Forex Broker
Forex Broker
17.1. Picking a Forex Broker (00:56)
17.2. Broker, Charting and Execution Software Example (02:22)

18. How to Place a Trade
Limit Entry Order
18.1. Buy Limit Entry Order (04:16)
18.2. Sell Limit Entry Order (03:53)

Limit Order
18.3. Buy Limit Order (03:39)

18.4. Sell Limit Order (02:46)

Stop Order
18.5. The Importance of Using Stops (01:05)
18.6. The Cardinal Rule on Stops (01:33)
18.7. Moving the Stop Order (00:46)
18.8. Be Patient and Leave Your Stop Alone (01:09)
18.9. Average Stop Order for the Majors (00:19)
18.10. Definition of Trailing Stop (00:57)
18.11. How to Place Trailing Stops (01:40)

19. How to Set up Your Charts
Charts Setup
19.1. IT Finance Charts Reference Guide Link (00:24)
19.2. Drawing Arrows on IT Finance Charts (00:14)
19.3. IT Finance Charts Custom Settings (00:36)
19.4. Using Templates on IT Finance Charts (01:07)
19.5. How to Simulate Real-Time Using IT Finance Charts (00:24)

20. How to Treat Demo Trading
Demo Trading
20.1. Trade in Your Sandbox Until You See a Trade (02:15)

Video CD Instructions

This course includes a set of Windows-based video CDs containing tutorials that provide additional explanation on concepts described in this manual.

These videos CDs will automatically play (autorun) on any Microsoft Windows system. Simply insert the CD into the CD/DVD player on your PC and a video menu will be displayed. Click on a video title to start playing.

Before We Begin

The Forexmentor course is designed and developed by experienced traders that were, at one time, just like you. We fully understand the rigors of the educational path you are embarking on. Additionally, we are aware of the pitfalls that many 'newbie' traders often fall into. Therefore, we will explain why some methods work well, why some methods work only at certain times and why others do not work at all for the Forex market.

At Forexmentor, we have a favorite saying: "If you think trading is *easy*, it will only get harder. If you think trading is *hard work*, it will only get *easier*."

Far too often, we see traders hastily learn a few concepts and start trading their hard-earned money. Learning to trade currencies takes hard work, commitment and guidance from those with trading experience. The bottom line is that if you do *not* know how the trading tools work and how to use them together, then *DO NOT trade your hard-earned money!*

The Holy Grail

Trying to find the '*Holy Grail*' of trading is a common pitfall of many traders. If you are a trader that is constantly in search of a new trading indicator, strategy or book that you think is finally going to give you the necessary skills to make money in the market, then you **are** on the 'Holy Grail' quest of trading.

There are over 200 technical trading indicators (not including custom designed ones). Many of these standard 200 indicators are merely variations of each other. If discretion is not exercised, you may find yourself jumping from indicator to indicator and just end up drowning in a 'sea of trading indicators'.

In this course, we will introduce you to only a handful of *proven* technical trading tools, we will demonstrate how they work and how you should use them.

This Manual

This course is presented in an "easy-to-read format". Another unique feature of this manual is that it is interactive. Each of the topics discussed in the manual have corresponding video tutorials that provide additional visual and audio explanations of the topic using examples from real Forex trading charts. Thus, you can not only read the information, but can also listen to Peter explain the topic in greater detail. By combining the printed material with the powers of the internet, your Forex learning experience is enhanced and truly unique.

The first section of this manual will focus on basic trading concepts and strategies. The second section will focus on the *application* of these concepts and strategies. In the third section, we will discuss Forex market essentials that are vital to your trading.

Color Charts: A note about the charts used in the manual. The charts reproduced in this manual are printed in black and white. However, all the charts are available in color online at – www.forexmentor.com/update/manual/. Simply go to this link and find the corresponding chart to view the color reproduction of the desired chart in greater detail. Please also visit: www.forementor.com/update/ to view other course updates and corrections.

Get Ready…

You are about to learn *proven* trading tools and strategies, used by professional traders, to take profits consistently from the Forex market !

Part I

Basic Technical Analysis Tools

How Price Moves

How does price move?

The answer is simple, yet a very powerful trading concept to keep in mind throughout your entire trading career. Price only moves in two directions, *UP* and *DOWN*. That's it!

Some will argue that price moves *sideways,* but it really does not. It is *time* that moves sideways. If you are looking at a price chart, time is always moving forward to the right but price only moves up or down.

Price has only two types of activities – Price is either *rallying* or *consolidating*.

When price moves up or down dramatically over a period of time (hours, days or weeks), we call this movement a *price rally*. Another term that traders use to describe this type of price movement is a "run". (See **HPAM1.0** for an example of a price rally)

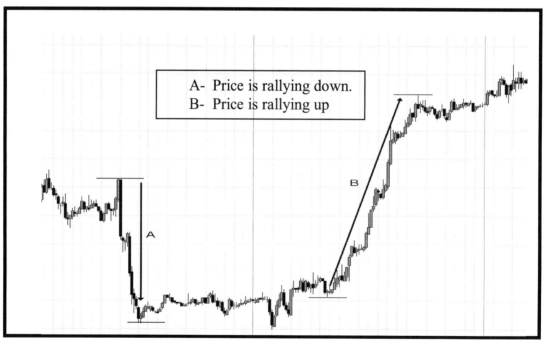

HPAM1.0 – Price Rallying UP and DOWN

22 How to Trade Currencies Like the 'Big Dogs'

Price may also move up or down in very small increments over a given period of time (few hours, days or weeks). We call this type of movement a *price consolidation*. Other terms traders use to describe price consolidation are: "price is stuck", "price is consolidating" or "price is moving sideways". (See **HPAM1.1** for an example of price consolidation)

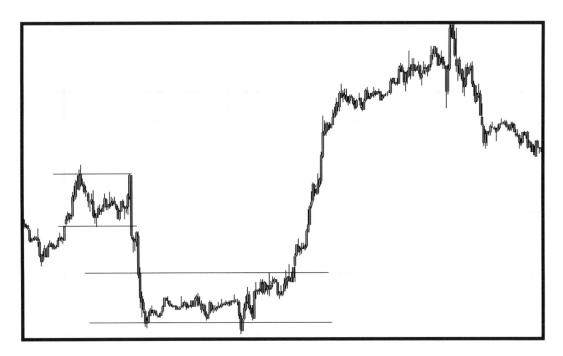

Summary: Price only moves in two directions; up or down. Price only has two activities – rallying or consolidating. When you read a price chart, always ask yourself: "Is price rallying or consolidating?"

How Price Moves

Personal Notes and Observations

Support and Resistance

Support and **Resistance** are the foundation upon which most technical analysis tools are based. Support and Resistance are *price levels* that buyers and sellers tend to respect.

Price action can either *rally* or *consolidate* between support and resistance. News agencies and newsletters will come up with reasons "why" a certain price level was respected. For now, you just need to know that these levels exist and be able to identify them. It is vital to your success as a trader to understand the concept of support and resistance.

As you start to examine price charts, you will notice that price moves across your charts in *waves*. Sometimes these waves appear to be moving *up;* sometimes they appear to be moving *down*. Other times they just seem to be moving *sideways*.

Whichever way they are moving, you will start to notice that price often likes to bounce between two levels: an *upper* level and a *lower* level. We call the upper level **RESISTANCE** and the lower level **SUPPORT**. The more technical definitions are:

RESISTANCE: A price level at which there are enough sellers and selling (downward) pressure that they create a strong enough force to overcome buyers and buying (upward) pressure so that the sellers are able to prevent price from going further upward.

SUPPORT: A price level at which there are enough buyers and buying (upward) pressure that they create a strong enough force to overcome sellers and selling (downward) pressure so that the buyers are able to prevent price from going further down.

Since resistance is the upper level you can think of it like a *ceiling*. What happens when you throw a ball against the ceiling? It bounces off and drops to the floor. If you have one of those really bouncy "super balls" and you slam it against the floor, where will it stop? It will stop when it hits the ceiling. After hitting the ceiling it will bounce back down to the floor. Now with this concept in mind, look at the following diagram **SR1.0**. Are you able to see what we are describing?

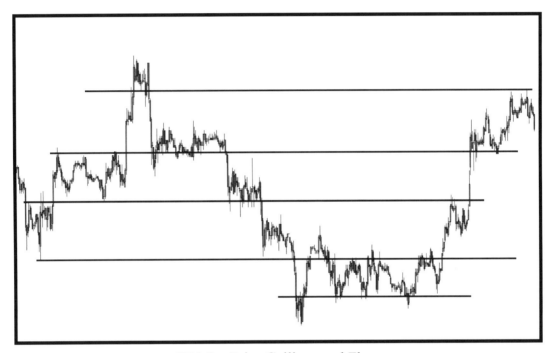

SR1.0 – Price Ceilings and Floors

Now let's take a moment and think about a building with many floors. If you were to fall through the floor (support), where would you land? On the next floor below you, right? And what would be your new ceiling (resistance)? It would be the floor that you just fell through (previous support), right?

Now if you bounce that "super" ball again, the old floor (previous support) would now be the ceiling (resistance), and the new floor would now be your floor (support). That is why you hear traders say: *support has now become resistance* or *resistance has now become support*. Let's take another look at diagram **SR1.1** and see if you can identify what we are talking about. Can you see where support *became* resistance and resistance *became* support?

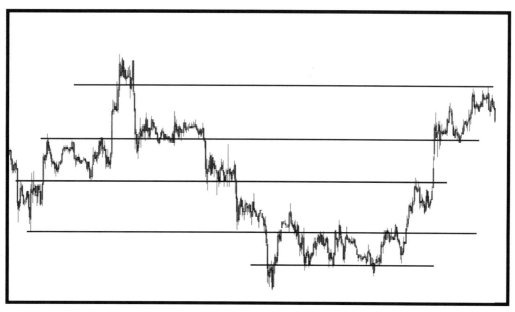

SR1.1 – Support Becomes Resistance, Resistance Becomes Support

Now, let's break down the chart into smaller chunks to make sure we thoroughly understand this concept of support and resistance.

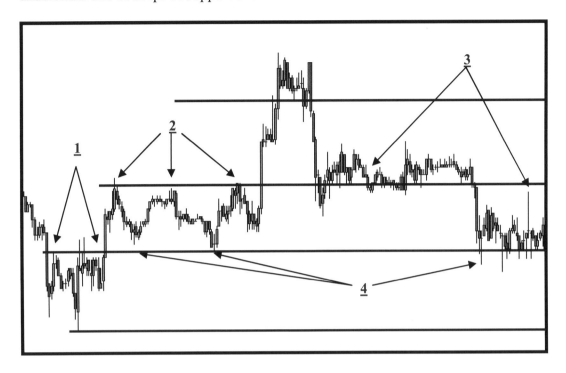

SR1.2 – Support and Resistance

Let's discuss the **SR1.2** diagram. Notice how price at **#1** was not able to break above that level. Several times, price went up to that level, which acted like a ceiling (resistance), and price bounced back down. When price did eventually break through the level at **#1**, it ran up to **#2** and bounced back down. Where did price bounce back down to? Price bounced back down to **#1** (previous ceiling), and is now acting like a *floor*. Price action was trapped between level **#1** and level **#2** for some time. Price came right up to the **#2** level three times before it was able to penetrate through it and move higher. After price did break through **#2** and ran up, where did it fall back to? It fell back to **#3**. So now **#2** (previous ceiling) is acting like a floor of support for price. Then when price action broke through the **#3** level it fell to **#4**, which was the old **#1** ceiling. Are you starting to understand this concept?

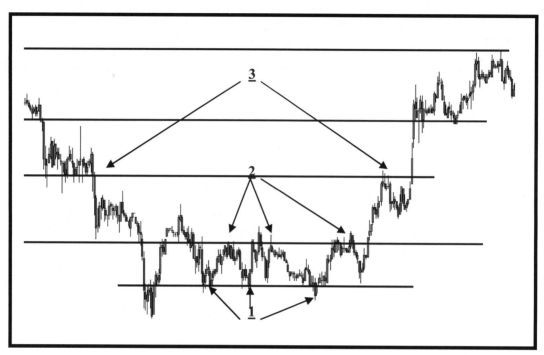

SR1.3 – Support and Resistance

In diagram **SR1.3**, price was, for the most part, contained between **#1** and **#2**. They were acting like a floor and a ceiling to price. Did you see that when price finally broke through the **#2** level, it ran to **#3** and stopped? Level **#3** had been a floor earlier, and even though that floor was from a previous time, it still acted as a ceiling to price in the future.

A key point to remember: **Levels of previous support or resistance, even though they may have occurred in the past, can still act as either support or resistance again in the future.**

Support and Resistance

Personal Notes and Observations

Price Patterns

Chart patterns are a pictorial way of viewing price action of a currency pair. There are many different price patterns and they can appear in any time frame. As with all other technical indicators, the higher the time frame they appear in, the more significant they are.

Although there are many price patterns, they can be divided into two categories: *Reversal Patterns* and *Continuation Patterns*. When looking for price patterns, one should keep in mind that "perfect" patterns seldom appear on charts. However, the experienced trader will be able to identify many "sloppy" versions of these patterns. The chart patterns that we will be discussing are:

1-2-3 Tops
1-2-3 Bottoms
Double Tops
Double Bottoms
Triple Tops
Triple Bottoms
Head and Shoulders
Inverted Head and Shoulders
Flags and Pennants
Symmetrical Triangles

Reversal Patterns

1-2-3 Tops

The 1-2-3 Top pattern appears when price runs up to a high, then pulls back down, and then makes another attempt to move higher. However, on the second run up, price fails to get as high as, or higher than the first high and when price breaks below the low of the pull back from the first high, the pattern is complete and we can anticipate a decline in price. (See diagram **CP1.0**)

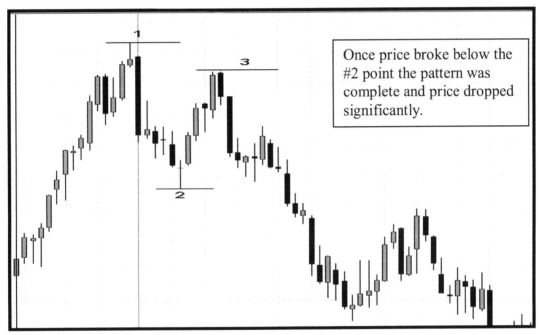

CP1.0 – 1-2-3 Top Pattern

1. Price Patterns
1-2-3 Tops

Refer to:
CD Disk 1

1.1. Identifying 1-2-3 Tops (01:08)
Peter explains what a 1-2-3 top looks like, where to enter on a 1-2-3 top and shows examples of 1-2-3 tops.

1.2. 1-2-3 Top Example (00:45)
An example of a 1-2-3 top on the EUR/USD hourly chart.

1-2-3 Bottoms

The 1-2-3 Bottom pattern is the reverse of the 1-2-3 Top pattern. This pattern appears when price runs down to a low, then pulls back up, and then makes another attempt to move lower. However, on the second run down price fails to get as low as, or lower than the first low and when price breaks above the high of the pull back up from the first low, the pattern is complete and we can anticipate an increase in price. (See diagram **CP1.1**)

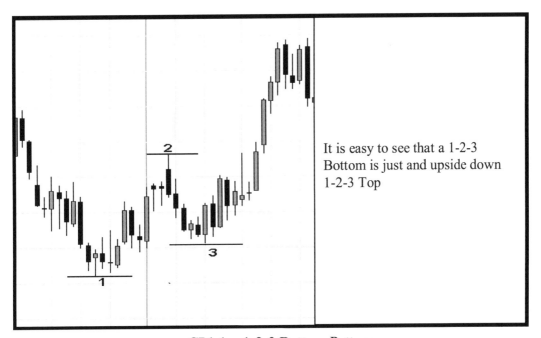

CP1.1 – 1-2-3 Bottom Pattern

1. Price Patterns
1-2-3 Bottoms

Refer to:
CD Disk 1

1.3. Identifying 1-2-3 Bottoms (02:23)
Peter explains what a 1-2-3 bottom looks like, where to enter on a 1-2-3 bottom and also shows examples of 1-2-3 bottoms.

1.4. What Does a 1-2-3 Bottom Look Like (00:42)
Peter uses a graphical representation of a 1-2-3 bottom and explains conceptually what a 1-2-3 bottom looks like. Also, Peter shows more examples of 1-2-3 bottoms

1.5. 1-2-3 Bottom Example (00:35)
An example of a 1-2-3 bottom on the EUR/USD 15 minute chart submitted by a Forexmentor member.

1.6. 1-2-3 Bottom Trading Example 1 (02:02)
Peter walks you through a trading scenario on the EUR/USD 5 minute chart in which a 1-2-3 bottom had formed and eventually resulted in a rise in price.

1.7. 1-2-3 Bottom Trading Example 2 (02:13)
A submission from a Forexmentor member who correctly identified a 1-2-3 bottom on the EUR/USD 5 minute chart which subsequently lead to a 23 pip gain.

Double Tops

The Double Tops pattern is identified when price makes a *new high* and then price retreats back down from the high. Price then rallies again in an attempt to break the previous high but cannot and then retreats. This is one of the most common patterns seen in currency trading so keep your eyes open for it.

Notice that in diagram **CP1.2**, price went up to **Point A**. After some time had passed, price then again went up to **Point B**, which was the same price level as **Point A**. Price could not penetrate the price level established at **Point A** and so after touching that level again at **Point B**, price fell back down significantly.

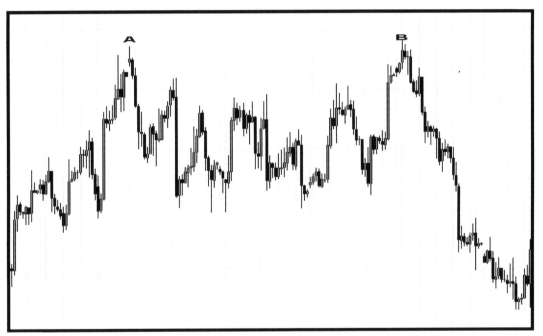

CP1.2 – Double Tops Pattern

1. Price Patterns
Double Tops

Refer to:
CD Disk 1

1.8. Double Top Example (00:35)
An example of a double top on the EUR/USD daily chart which eventually resulted in a significant fall in price.

Double Bottoms

The Double Bottoms pattern is the reverse of the Double Tops pattern. This pattern is identified when price makes a *new low* and then price pulls back up from the low. Price then attempts to break the previous low but cannot and then pulls back up. This is also one of the most common patterns seen in currency trading so keep you eyes open for it.

In diagram **CP1.3**, we have an example of two double bottoms: **A-B** which happened to occur very close to each other, and **C-D** which happened to occur after a large time interval. The point to keep in mind is that whether the double bottoms are close together or farther apart, you should be keeping your eyes on a price level that price has backed off from, when it reaches there again.

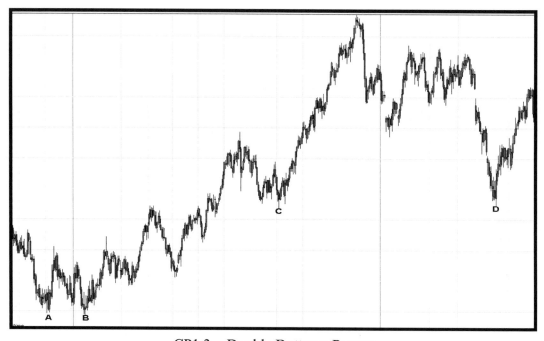

CP1.3 – Double Bottoms Pattern

1. Price Patterns
Double Bottoms

Refer to:
CD Disk 1

1.9. Double Bottom Example (00:42)
An example of a double bottom on the USD/CHF 15 & 5 minute chart.

Triple Tops and Triple Bottoms

Triple tops are like their relatives the double tops, except that price makes a third attempt at taking out the previous high but gets rejected. Triple bottoms are like their relative the double bottoms, except that price make a third attempt at taking out the previous low but gets rejected. Since triple tops and triple bottoms are rare, the price move after a triple top or a triple bottom occurrence is usually quite significant. (See diagram **CP1.4**)

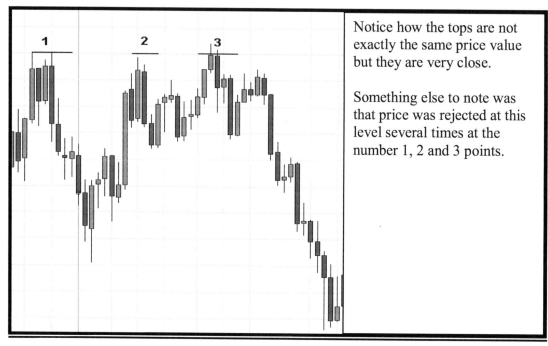

CP1.4 – Triple Tops Pattern

Head and Shoulders

The components of the head and shoulders pattern are the *three peaks* and its *neckline*. To form this pattern, price first rises to a peak and then pulls back down (**Point A**). Second, price then rallies above the previous high and creates a new *higher* high (**Point B**) and then pulls back again. Third, price again attempts to rally to (**Point C**), which is a failed attempt at achieving the same high as the second peak (**Point B**), and then pulls back down again. When price breaks the neckline (**Line D**) of the head and shoulders, the pattern is said to be complete. Many times on the third rally up, (Point C) will reach the price level of the first rally, (Point A), but not always. (See diagram **CP1.5**)

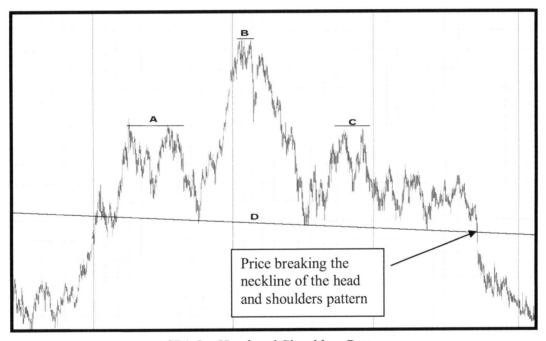

CP1.5 – Head and Shoulders Pattern

1. Price Patterns
Head and Shoulders

Refer to:
CD Disk 1

1.10. Head and Shoulders Example 1 (02:26)
An example of a head and shoulders on the EUR/USD 15 minute chart.

1.11. Head and Shoulders Example 2 (00:39)
An example of a head and shoulders on the EUR/USD 15 minute chart.

1.12. Head and Shoulders Example 3 (00:42)
Peter reviews a submission from a Forexmentor member regarding an example of a head and shoulders pattern on the EUR/JPY daily chart.

1.13. Head and Shoulders Examples (00:19)
Two more examples of a head and shoulders pattern on the EUR/USD and EUR/JPY pair.

1.14. How to Trade a Head and Shoulders (00:27)
Using the USD/CHF 5 minute chart, Peter explains how to trade a head and shoulders

Inverted Head and Shoulders

The components of the inverted head and shoulders pattern are the *three lows* and its *neckline*. To form this pattern, price first falls to a low and then pulls back up (**Point A**). Second, price then rallies back down below the previous low and creates a new *lower* low (**Point B**) and then pulls back up again. Third, price again attempts to rally down to (**Point C**), which is a failed attempt at achieving the same low as (**Point B**) and pulls back up again. When price breaks the neckline (**Line D**) of the inverted head and shoulders, the pattern is said to be complete. Many times on the third rally down, (Point C) will reach the price level of the first rally down, (Point A), but not always. (See diagram **CP1.6**)

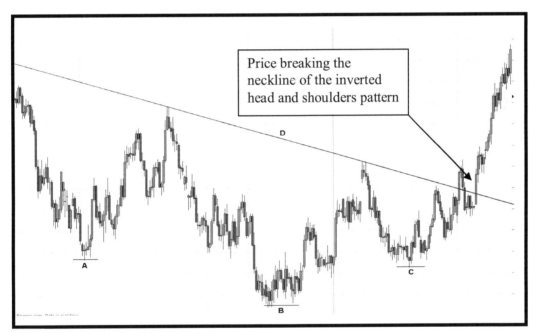

CP1.6 – Inverted Head and Shoulders Patterns

1. Price Patterns
<u>Inverted Head and Shoulders</u>

Refer to:
CD Disk 1

1.15. Inverted Head and Shoulders Example (01:32)
An example of an inverted head and shoulders on the EUR/USD 15 minute chart.

Continuation Patterns

A continuation pattern develops because price has recently rallied and needs to take a *break* before continuing on with a much larger rally. Price rarely, if ever, continues to run, and run in one direction.

Flags

Flags are patterns that develop when price takes a break before continuing in the same direction as it was going before the flag pattern appeared. The rally up before the flag is considered the *flag pole*. The *bull flag* in an uptrend sometimes goes straight sideways or slopes downward against the uptrend before breaking back upwards. (See diagram **CP1.7**)

CP1.7 – Bull Flag Pattern

1. Price Patterns
Bull Flags

Refer to:
CD Disk 1

1.16. Bull Flag Example 1 (00:15)
An example of a bull flag in an uptrend on the EUR/USD daily chart. Bull flags are also known as channels.

1.17. Bull Flag Example 2 (00:40)
An example of a bull flag in an uptrend on the USD/JPY 5 minute chart. Bull flags are also known as channels.

1.18. Bull Flag in an Uptrend (01:31)
What do you see? Peter sees a bull flag in an uptrend on the EUR/USD daily chart.

The *bear flag* in a downtrend sometimes goes straight sideways or slopes upward against the downtrend before breaking back downwards. (See diagram **CP1.8**)

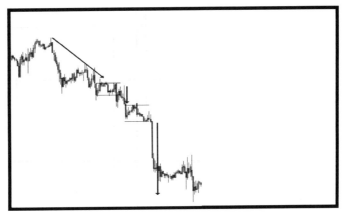

CP1.8 – Bear Flag Pattern

1. Price Patterns
Bear Flags

Refer to:
CD Disk 1

1.19. Bear Flag Example 1 (00:23)
An example of a bear flag in a downtrend on the EUR/USD 15 minute chart. Bear flags are also known as channels.

1.20. Bear Flag Example 2 (00:23)
Examples of bear flags in a downtrend on the EUR/USD and GBP/USD 15 minute chart. Bear flags are also known as channels.

1.21. Bear Flag in a Downtrend (01:27)
Peter describes another version of a bear flag in a downtrend using the GBP/USD daily chart.

1.22. How to Plot a Flag (00:39)
Peter explains how to plot a flag, also known as a channel, in an uptrend.

Pennants

Pennants are patterns characterized by having one fairly even and straight side and another sloping side. They, like the flag, develop when price takes a *break* before continuing on in the same direction it was going before the pennant pattern appeared. The rally up before the pennant pattern is considered the pole of the pennant. Pennants are closely related to the flag pattern and sometimes turn into a flag because price action expands a bit. (See diagram **CP1.9**)

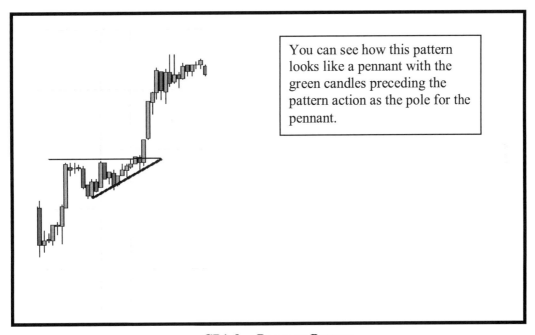

CP1.9 – Pennant Pattern

Triangles

Triangles can be a bit tricky because they can *either* be a continuation pattern or a reversal pattern. It is recommended that beginning traders take caution when trading triangle breakouts. Many times a triangle pattern will have a quick, fast break out in one direction that is *false,* and very quickly rebound and break out for real in the opposite direction.

Triangles come in several different types: *ascending, descending, symmetrical* and *expanding*. We have provided you with a few examples of symmetrical triangles, the most common triangles that you will see appear, that were both continuation patterns and reversal patterns. (See diagrams **CP1.10** & **CP1.11**)

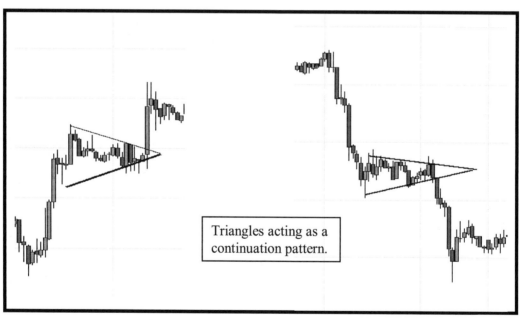

CP 1.10 – Symmetrical Triangle Pattern

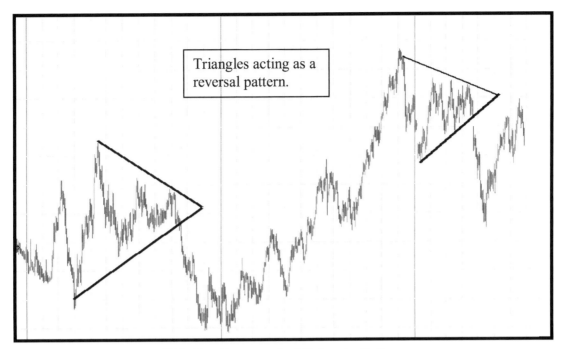

CP1.11 – Symmetrical Triangle Pattern

It is good to *memorize* what these patterns look like and practice finding and drawing them on your charts. Your first goal should be to recognize chart patterns quickly and know whether or not they are a reversal or continuation pattern. Second, you should be able to see them as price starts to form them, so that you can anticipate how they should be traded.

There are more chart patterns in the technical analysis world. Our intent was to introduce you to the most common chart patterns that you will encounter. For a more exhaustive discussion on chart patterns, a good website to go to is: www.chartpatterns.com.

1. Price Patterns
Triangles in an Uptrend

Refer to:
CD Disk 1

1.23. Triangle Example 1 (00:28)
An example of a triangle in an uptrend on the EUR/USD 15 minute chart.

1.24. Triangle Example 2 (01:03)
An example of a triangle in an uptrend on the EUR/USD pair.

1.25. Triangle Example 3 (01:29)
An example of a triangle in an uptrend on the EUR/USD 30 minute chart submitted by a Forexmentor member.

1.26. Triangle Trading Example (00:39)
An example of a triangle in an uptrend on the EUR/USD 15 minute chart submitted by a Forexmentor member. Profit for the day based on the breakout of the triangle was 31 pips.

1. Price Patterns
Triangles in an Downtrend

Refer to:
CD Disk 1

1.27. Triangle Example 1 (00:29)
An example of a triangle in a downtrend on the EUR/USD hourly & 15 minute chart.

1.28. Triangle Example 2 (00:34)
An example of a triangle in a downtrend on the EUR/USD daily chart.

1.29. Triangle Example 3 (01:48)
An example of a triangle in a downtrend on the EUR/USD 15 minute chart that came to fruition with price collapsing after breaking out of the triangle.

1.30. Triangle Example 4 (02:22)
An example of a triangle in a downtrend on the EUR/USD daily chart that came to fruition with price collapsing after breaking out of the triangle.

1.31. Triangle Example 5 (00:32)
An example of a triangle in a downtrend on the EUR/USD 15 minute chart submitted by a Forexmentor member

1.32. Triangle Example 6 (01:19)
Two examples of triangles, one in an uptrend and one in a downtrend on the EUR/USD 15 minute chart. Both triangles came to fruition.

1.33. Triangle Trading Example (01:00)
An example of a triangle in a downtrend on the EUR/USD 15 minute chart submitted by a Forexmentor member. Profit for the day based on the breakout of the triangle was 44 pips.

1.34. How to Draw Triangles (01:00)
Peter shows you a simple method on how to draw triangles on price.

Price Patterns

Personal Notes and Observations

Pivot Points

Pivot Points are the essential element of Peter Bain & Forexmentor's technical analysis course and studies. Pivot Points are, at their simplest, points of support and resistance. What makes them important is that they are mathematically calculated points of support and resistance that the 'Big Dogs' use for trading every day. This fact raises their significance above "just being support and resistance" levels. Wouldn't it be important to you to know that a certain price level is also a Pivot Point level? Would the fact that a support or resistance level on the chart is also a Pivot Point be significant? The answer is "YES!" to both questions.

Before the common use of calculators, computers, and internet connections, trading was done by people in 'pits' shouting and waving at each other with crazy hand signals to communicate buy and sell orders. These traders developed some simple calculations based on the *previous* day's price action to help them anticipate today's price action. They would carry around these values on little pieces of paper and when price action reached one of these values, they would execute some type of trading order accordingly. These calculations are what we refer to *as Pivot Points*.

Refer to:
CD Disk 2

2. Pivot Points
Pivot Points

2.1. Pivot Points Origin (00:43)
Pivot points originated in the pits in Chicago; in the future pits. Floor traders would write the pivot levels on the back of their trading cards and buy or sell accordingly.

2.2. Pivot Points Overview 1 (03:44)
When looking at a chart with just price action plotted, it's pretty difficult to gauge where price action is going when you don't have any points of reference. Pivot points offer up significant support and resistance levels in which now a trader can use to make an intelligent trading decision.

2.3. Pivot Points Overview 2 (02:47)
It's pretty hard to trade a chart with just price action plotted without any points of reference. The solution is pivot points; allowing you to draw reference points on your chart to help you gauge where price is going.

2.4. Pivot Points Overview 3 (02:03)
You wouldn't play football on a field without lines. Why would you trade the Forex without pivot points?

We will now discuss the *nine* pivot point levels, their calculations, and how they look on a price chart.

The first calculation was the *Central Pivot Point*. It is the *average* of yesterday's Open, High, Low and Close prices. This pivot is expected to be the *midpoint* of today's trading range, unless price is pushed beyond yesterday's range by some fundamental factor or global disaster. So, if price is above the Central Pivot, it is likely that price will come down to it and if price is below than the Central Pivot, it is likely to come up to the Central Pivot. (See diagram **PP1.0**)

WARNING: This is how price will move often. However, sometimes the trend will be overpowering and price will NOT go back to the Central Pivot. New traders often want to know why this happens. The answer is; it just does. Nothing in trading works 100% of the time. Remember that, it will serve you well in your trading career. The key is not to be frustrated when it does not work. Just accept it and be happy that you have a tool that works a high percentage of the time.

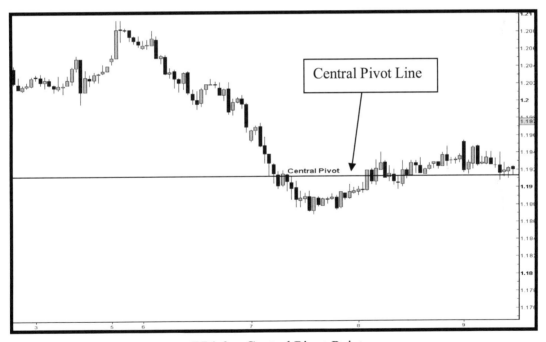

PP1.0 – Central Pivot Point

In diagram **PP1.0**, you can see the Central Pivot line that was obtained for the trading session starting March 8th. Price started out below the Central Pivot and over the course of the trading session moved up towards it. As price moved above the Central

Pivot, notice how it used that value as a floor for support. Price continually came down to the price level of the Central Pivot and bounced off of it. If you did not know about pivot points, how would you have known why price was finding support at such an odd place? Does it help to know what the 'Big Dogs' know?

The pivot point calculations are to determine **Support** and **Resistance** levels. These calculations are based off the value generated for the Central Pivot. On days where there is NOT an extremely strong trend in place, S1 (support level 1) and R1 (resistance level 1) are price levels that a trader would expect price to reach, then turn around and head back towards the Central Pivot. For days with a stronger trend, S2 (support level 2) and R2 (resistance level 2) are also calculated giving traders a set of *five* pivot points: S2, S1, Central Pivot, R1, R2. (See diagram **PP1.1**)

PP1.1 – S2, S1, Central Pivot, R1, R2 Pivot Points

In diagram **PP1.1**, were you able to notice how price was contained by R1? It acted like a ceiling of resistance not letting price pass through it, forcing it to bounce on the floor of the support level of the Central Pivot point.

Some traders wonder why these pivots work so well and continue to work so well. It is because the use of these pivot points has become so *universal* that they have become a major influence on market sentiment and expectations affecting trader behavior as price approaches the pivots. Some argue that they are a 'self-fulfilling prophecy'. Whether that is the case or not, the bottom line is that they work, and should be what concerns us the most. Also adding to the impact of the pivots are the many computerized trading programs that make automated buys and sells based on the inclusion of these pivot points. That is why you MUST know about pivot points and how price reacts to them.

JUST A NOTE: Trading literature is full of other support and resistance tools: Fibonacci lines, Gann fans, Moving Averages and references to historic highs and lows. On a daily basis, these are all less reliable than the pivot calculations for the Forex market. That is not to say that they do not add value to your trading, but they assume that the market will repeat itself based on fixed intervals, linear analysis and have a static view of the market. Forex markets are very dynamic and traders are better served by pivot points, which are based on a very recent time period and used by the 'Big Dogs'.

Currencies usually trend and the original *five* pivot levels we have discussed thus far need a bit more refinement. So Peter developed four other price levels, which he has named M1, M2, M3 and M4. That brings the total number of pivot points at your disposal to *nine*. Adding these pivot levels gives us a more clear view of price action. They also allow you to see price movement with clearly defined markers, like you would see on a football field. (See diagram **PP1.2**)

PP1.2 – M1, M2, M3 & M4 Pivot Points

In diagram **PP1.2**, we now have the *M level* pivot points added. Even though R1 contained price as noted earlier in diagram **PP1.1**, notice how helpful it was to know about the special M3 pivot that Peter developed. Could you be more successful in your trading knowing what the 'Big Dogs' know?

2. Pivot Points
Pivot Points

Refer to:
CD Disk 2

2.5. Marking Pivot Points on Charts (04:30)
Peter shows you how to plot pivot points on the EUR/USD 15 minute chart.

How to Calculate the Pivots

You will find it easier to use the 60 minute chart to work with when getting the values for the pivot calculations. Forexmentor works with *midnight* to *midnight* Eastern Standard Time to obtain the values used in the pivot calculations. Using this time frame will generate results that allow you to study the market 3 hours before the London market open (the largest market in the world), to prepare your trading plans for the upcoming days trading session.

Of course you can base the calculations on any time zone or time period you wish but Forexmentor uses midnight to midnight EST for its published pivot points (member area). You may wish to consider recalculating the pivot points after price action has moved an extreme amount during one session (the main sessions being London, New York and Asia).

Refer to:
CD Disk 2

2. Pivot Points
How to Calculate the Pivots

2.6. Calculating Pivot Points Overview 1 (02:42)
The pivot points posted every Tuesday to Friday in the Forexmentor member's area are calculated from midnight to midnight EST; 3 hours in advance of the London open. You may choose to recalculate your pivot points for the NY Session or the Asian Session.

2.7. Calculating Pivot Points Overview 2 (04:51)
The pivot points posted every Tuesday to Friday in the Forexmentor member's area are calculated from midnight to midnight EST; 3 hours in advance of the London open. You may choose to recalculate your pivot points for the NY Session or the Asian Session.

2.8. Posting of Pivot Points (00:24)
Here is the link to the daily pivot points posted every Tuesday to Friday for seven major currency pairs in the Forexmentor member's area.

2.9. Projected Range and Actual Range (01:33)
Peter explains how the projected range and actual range values are

calculated which are published along with the daily pivot points in the Forexmentor member's area.

2.10. Recalculating Pivot Points 1 (02:55)
Peter suggests some key times in which one can consider recalculating your pivot points depending on which session you choose to trade.

2.11. Recalculating Pivot Points 2 (01:35)
Peter suggests some key times in which one can consider recalculating your pivot points after price action has moved an extreme amount during one session.

Now let's go over how to obtain the values used in calculating pivot points:

1. Open a 60 minute chart.

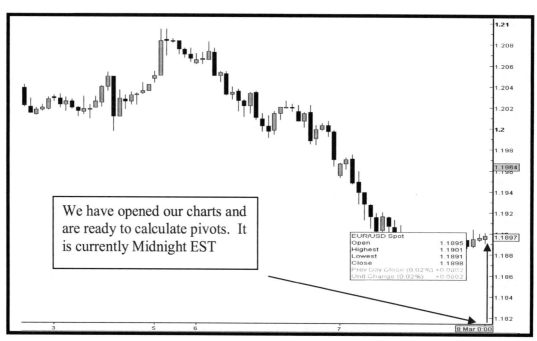

PP1.3 – Midnight EST

2. To find the 'OPEN' value for the calculations, move your cursor back in time until you find the 12 AM candle from the previous day. (If it is now the 8th of March EST, you will be looking for the 12 AM EST March 7th candle). The opening price for that candle will be your 'OPEN' price needed for the calculations. (See diagram **PP1.4**)

Notice in the drawing that the crosshairs on the March 7th midnight candle and the 'OPEN' price for that candle was 1.1955. This is the value you would use for the *OPEN* price in your pivot calculations.

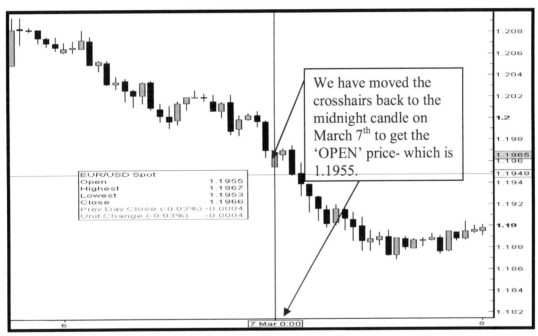

PP1.4 – Open Value

3. Next you will look for the *highest* high and the *lowest* low that price went to between the March 7th 12 AM candle and the March 8th 12 AM candle. The highest high that price went to will be your 'HIGH' value for the pivot calculations and the lowest low will be your 'LOW' for the pivot calculations.

In **PP1.5**, notice that the highest high, the candle with the crosshairs on it, was at 2 AM on March 7th, giving us a price of 1.1975 for our *HIGH* value for the pivot calculations.

PP1.5 – High Value

In **PP1.6,** notice that the lowest low, the candle with the crosshairs on it, was at 14:00 on March 7th, giving us the price of 1.1869 for our *LOW* value for the pivot calculations.

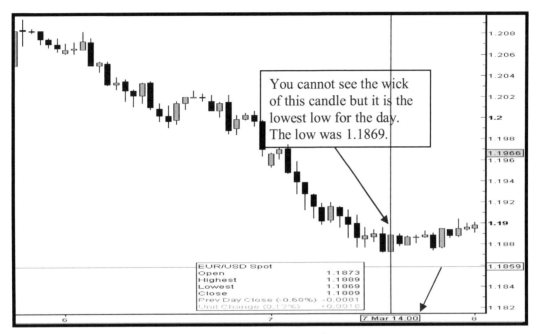

PP1.6 – Low Value

4. Finally, go to the current 12 AM candle for March 8th. Obtain its *opening* price as noted in diagram **PP1.7**. That will be your *CLOSE* value for the pivot calculations.

Since there is no official opening and closing of the Forex market, the absolute last price dealt will most closely be represented by the opening of the 12 AM candle for March 8th, instead of the closing price of the 11PM candle for March 7th. That may sound a bit confusing, but after you have done it a few hundred times you won't even have to think about it.

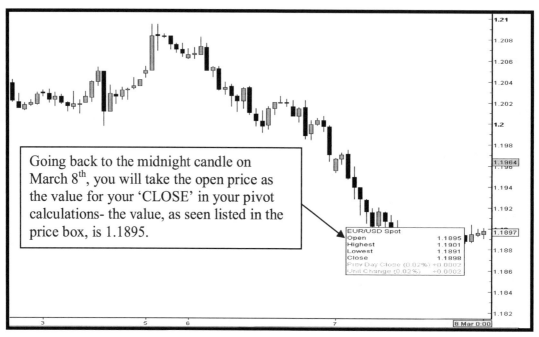

PP1.7 – Close Value

Now that you have these values, you can go to the following link at the Forexmentor website to calculate the pivot points:

http://www.forexmentor.com/protect/pivot.php

Diagram **PP1.8** shows the upper portion of the pivot calculator with our values.

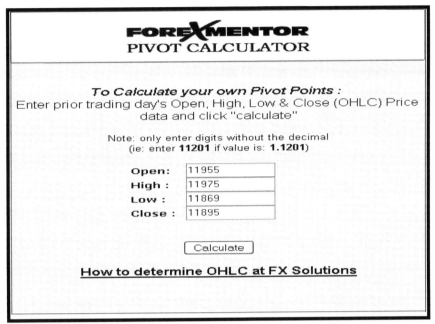

PP1.8 – Pivot Calculator with Values Inserted

Diagram **PP1.9** shows the lower portion of the pivot calculator with the calculated pivot values.

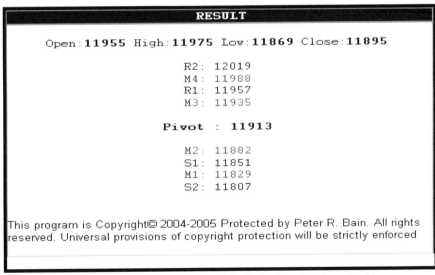

PP1.9 – Pivot Calculator with Calculated Pivot Values

This is how the pivots would look if we were to draw lines for all of the pivot values on our chart. (See diagram **PP1.10**)

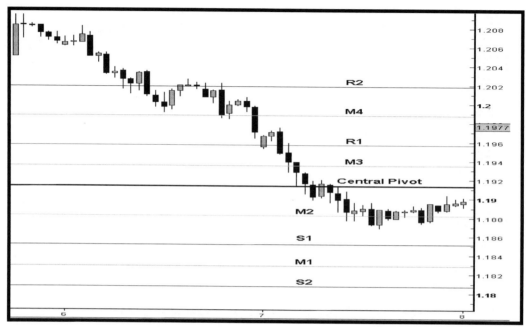

PP1.10 – All Nine Pivot Points Plotted

Refer to:
CD Disk 2

2. Pivot Points
How to Calculate the Pivots

2.12. Calculating Daily Pivot Points 1 (00:48)
Peter uses a conceptual diagram and explains how to calculate the midnight to midnight EST daily point points.

2.13. Calculating Daily Pivot Points 2 (11:10)
An example of how to calculate daily pivot points on the hourly chart for the EUR/USD pair.

2.14. Calculating Pivots Points Using the Daily Chart (01:39)
Peter explains why we suggest using the hourly chart when calculating pivot points instead of the daily chart.

Now let's look at how the pivots worked out in diagram **PP1.11**. When we calculated out pivots earlier, price was at M2. It then moved up out of the sell area of the pivots to M3, pulled back a bit and then slowly worked its way up to R1. What you should notice is that the pivots were like resting places for price as it moved up.

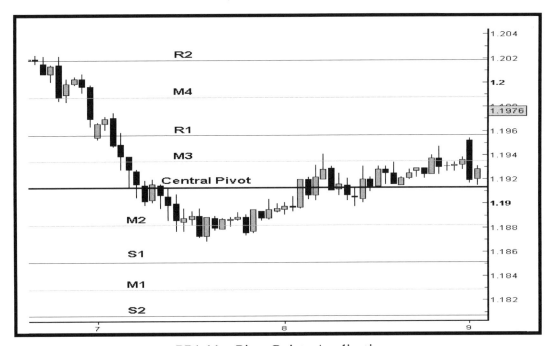

PP1.11 – Pivot Points Application

Pivot points can also be calculated to obtain *weekly*, *monthly* and *yearly* pivots. Using these longer time frame pivots is based on the trading style of the trader.

Refer to:
CD Disk 2

2. Pivot Points
How to Calculate the Pivots

2.15. Calculating Weekly Pivot Points 1 (00:58)
Peter uses a conceptual diagram and explains how to calculate the Sunday midnight to Sunday midnight EST weekly point points.

2.16. Calculating Weekly Pivot Points 2 (08:33)
An example of how to calculate weekly pivot points on the hourly chart for the EUR/USD pair.

2.17. Calculating Monthly and Yearly Pivot Points (00:19)
Information on how to calculate monthly and yearly pivot points on any currency pair.

It should also be noted that there are *several* methods for calculating pivots over weekends and holidays, but there is no consistently reliable method for doing so. This would be another area that is left to the discretion and trading style of the trader.

Refer to:
CD Disk 2

2. Pivot Points
How to Calculate the Pivots

2.18. Calculating Monday Pivot Points 1 (01:16)
Peter uses a conceptual diagram and explains one method on how to calculate point points for Monday.

2.19. Calculating Monday Pivot Points 2 (05:24)
An example of one method on how to calculate Monday pivot points on the hourly chart for the EUR/USD pair.

2.20. Calculating Holiday Pivot Points (06:44)
An example of one method on how to calculate pivot points after a holiday long weekend on the hourly chart for the EUR/USD pair.

How to Use the Pivot Points

When price is in or at the pivot points above the Central Pivot, price is considered to be in the *sell area* and we should look for other technical indicators to support going *short* the currency pair we are looking at. When price is in or at the pivot points below the Central Pivot, price is considered to be in the *buy area* and we should look for other technical indicators to support going *long* the currency pair we are looking at. (See diagram **PP1.12**) This diagram is a visual reminder of how the pivots should be traded to create the highest probability trades.

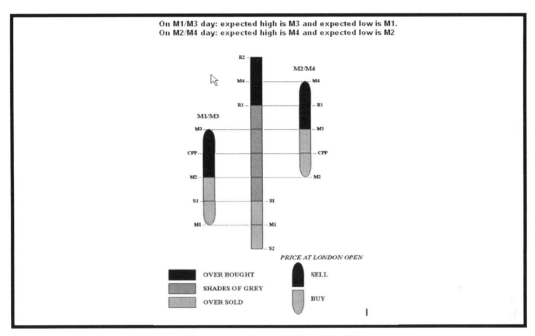

PP1.12 – Overbought/Oversold Areas

When price is between pivot points, it is considered to be in 'no man's land'. This means that it is usually an uncertain price at which to enter into a trade. Not that you need to wait until price is right on a pivot point to enter a trade, but in most cases, it is best to wait until price is at least close to a pivot point before considering placing a trade.

It should also be noted that in most cases the Central Pivot is also considered 'no man's land'. That means it would be a rare occurrence that we would want to get into a trade at that level because it is neither in the buy or sell area of the pivots. As always, there are exceptions to this guideline. However, newer traders should follow this guideline until they are able to clearly see a high probability trade at the Central Pivot.

Refer to:
CD Disk 2

2. Pivot Points
How to Use the Pivot Points

2.21. Pivot Points and Bias 1 (01:43)
Peters reviews the diagram PP1.12. which is a visual reminder of how the pivots should be traded to create the highest probability trades.

2.22. Pivot Points and Bias 2 (03:25)
Using the diagram PP1.12, Peter reiterates that the pivot "rules" are just guidelines. Nothing is cast in stone. At times, you may consider buying in a sell area and consider selling in a buy area.

2.23. Pivot Points and Bias 3 (01:36)
Peter reiterates that the pivot "rules" are just guidelines. Nothing is cast in stone. At times, you may consider buying in a sell area and consider selling in a buy area.

2.24. Pivots Points Trading Example 1 (02:36)
An example of how to trade pivots on the EUR/USD 15 minute chart.

2.25. Pivots Points Trading Example 2 (00:48)
An example of how to trade pivots on the EUR/JPY 15 minute chart.

2.26. Trading on Pivot Points Retest (02:51)
Using a conceptual diagram, Peter suggests another method on how pivot points can be traded. You want to buy/sell accordingly when price re-tests a pivot point.

The Pivot Points also have a repetitive pattern that occurs and when supported by other technical indicators are very nice to consider trading. It is referred to as the *M1/M3* and the *M2/M4* paradigm. This paradigm is determined by the difference between the open price of the 12am Eastern Time candle from today and the open price of the 12am Eastern Time candle from yesterday. If the open price of the 12am candle from today's session is *greater* or *higher* than the open price of the 12am candle from yesterday, then it is considered to be an *M2/M4 day*. If the open price of the 12am candle from today's session is *lesser* or *lower* than the open price of the 12am candle from yesterday, then it is considered to be an M1/M3 day. When it is an M1/M3 day, we anticipate that once price has reached M1, price will then look to find M3, and if price first had reached M3, price will then look to find M1. The M2/M4 day works just as the M1/M3 day works. This paradigm works about 50% of the time. You can increase this probability by learning how to integrate the use of other technical indicators when deciding whether or not to make this trade.

2. Pivot Points
M1/M3, M2/M4 Paradigm

Refer to:
CD Disk 2

2.27. M1/M3, M2/M4 Paradigm Explained 1 (04:45)
Using an example of the daily pivots posted in the Forexmentor members area in which the M1/M3, M2/M4 notations are included, the M1/M3, M2/M4 paradigm is explained.

2.28. M1/M3, M2/M4 Paradigm Explained 2 (01:02)
Peter explains the M1/M3, M2/M4 paradigm.

2.29. M1/M3, M2/M4 Paradigm Clarified 1 (00:59)
When a day is deemed M1/M3, it does not mean it will be a bearish day. When a day is deemed M2/M4, it does not mean it will be a bullish day. M1/M3 or M2/M4 is just the expect high/low for that particular day.

2.30. M1/M3, M2/M4 Paradigm Clarified 2 (01:15)
More often then not, one of the two levels will play out but not necessarily both. For example, for a day deemed M2/M4, price may find support at M2 but price may not necessarily find a high at M4.

2.31. M1/M3, M2/M4 Paradigm Clarified 3 (01:38)
More often then not, one of the two levels will play out but not necessarily both. For example, for a day deemed M1/M3, price may seek out M3 and find resistance but not necessarily find a low at M1.

2.32. M2/M4 Example (01:44)
An example of the M2/M4 paradigm playing out with price finding a low at M2 and a high at M4 on the GBP/USD 15 minute chart.

Hopefully you are starting to understand why Pivot Points are so important to know about when you are learning to trade. Your understanding of their importance will only grow as you gain experience in using them.

Pivot Points

Personal Notes and Observations

Candlesticks

Components of a Candlestick

There are many charting formats that a trader can use; line charts, bar charts, point figure charts and candlestick charts. While every format has its pros and cons, this course will *focus* on the candlestick charts and their usefulness. The components of an individual candlestick are noted in the diagram **CS1.0**. Candlestick charts can be based on any time frame chart you wish to look at; a 5 minute chart, a 15 minute chart, a 60 minute chart, a daily chart, etc. A candle will represent a period of the corresponding chart time frame you are examining.

For example, if you are looking at a 15 minute chart, one candle will represent 15 minutes. The top of the wick will represent the *highest* price dealt in that 15 minute period, and the tail will represent the *lowest* price dealt during that 15 minute period. The larger colored, rectangular area is referred to as the *candle body*. The body of the candle is the distance between the price dealt at the opening of the given 15 minute period and the price dealt at the closing of the 15 minute period.

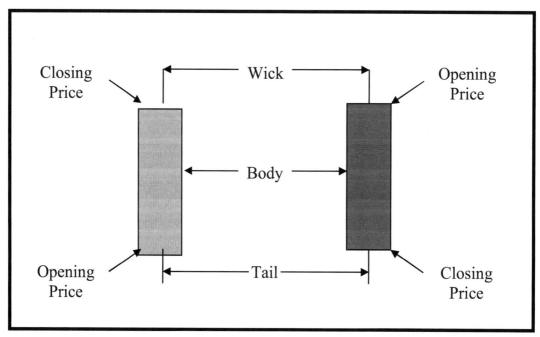

CS1.0 – Components of a Candlestick

(Note: Candlestick on left has green body. Candlestick on right has red body.)
If you will notice, in this example **CS1.0**, we have a green candle and a red candle. For our discussion today, the green candle is a candle that identifies price at the end

of the 15 minute period was higher than at the beginning of the 15 minute period; it can also be called a "bullish" or "upward" candle. The red candle tells us that price at the end of the 15 minute period was lower than the price at the beginning of the 15 minute period. It can also be called a "bearish" or "downward" candle. (It should be noted that most charting software packages will allow you to choose the color you want to represent the bullish and bearish candles. We could easily have chosen blue for the bullish candle and black for the bearish candle). The instant advantage that can be seen from using candles is that you can visually note very quickly whether price is either moving up or down. As you will soon see, this is just one thing that candles can tell you visually very quickly.

Refer to:
CD Disk 3

3. Candlesticks
Components of a Candlestick

3.1. Constructing Candlesticks (00:30)
Peter explains the body of the candle, the shadow/wicks of a candle, and the open and close prices for a candle.

Types of Candlesticks

There are many types of individual candlesticks. They are identified by specific names. There are also candlestick patterns, which are created by combining different types of individual candlesticks (we will learn about these in a bit). For now, let's just review the different types of individual candlesticks.

The Doji
(Neutral or Reversal Candle)

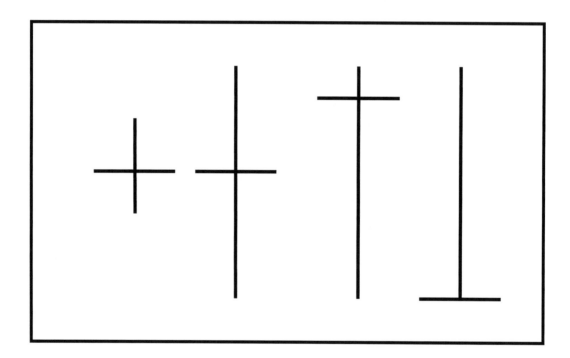

The "perfect" doji has no body, just a thin line to show that the opening and closing price of the time frame being analyzed were exactly the same. (It is important to remember that finding perfection in the markets is rare.) Most traders find it is acceptable for a doji to have a small body, very small. The length of their wicks and tails can vary.

By itself, a doji is a *neutral* candle. It shows us that neither buyers nor sellers have had an advantage to move price in their direction. It basically tells us that the struggle between the buyers and sellers ended in a tie for the time frame of the chart we are looking at. If we are an economist, we can say that a doji represents a relationship between supply and demand that is balanced.

The neutral status of the doji changes depending on the trend or candles that come before you see the doji on the chart. If a doji appears after a trend that is moving either up or down, it then starts to take on significance.

Let's say that price has been trending up and there are several large green candles and then a doji appears. In this scenario the buyers have had the advantage because demand has been *greater* than the available supply. The appearance of the doji tells us that price, for the moment, has become balanced. Price may still continue in an uptrend, however, the doji is a warning that price may now reverse and go the other way. (See diagram **CS1.1**)

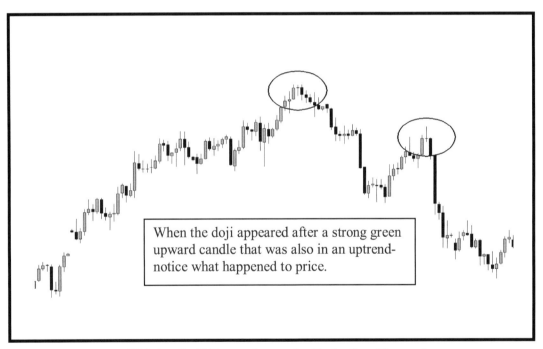

CS1.1 – Doji Examples at the End of an Uptrend

In the above examples, notice how both uptrends ended with a doji that was followed by a significant reversal in price. You can also find other doji in the chart where price did not reverse, why is that? Again, a doji is a neutral candle unless it occurs with *other* components of technical analysis. The combining of several components of technical analysis is called a "confluence of events". We will learn more about this later.

WARNING: There are many traders that have and will continue to take a trade in the opposite direction of a trend, based solely on the appearance of a doji. Do NOT do this. (See diagram **CS1.3**)

Now let's say that price has been trending down and there are several large red candles and then a doji appears. In this scenario the sellers have had the advantage because supply has been greater than the current demand. The appearance of the doji tells us that price, for the moment, has become balanced. Price may still continue in a downtrend, however, the doji is a warning that prices may now reverse and go the other way. (See diagram **CS1.2**)

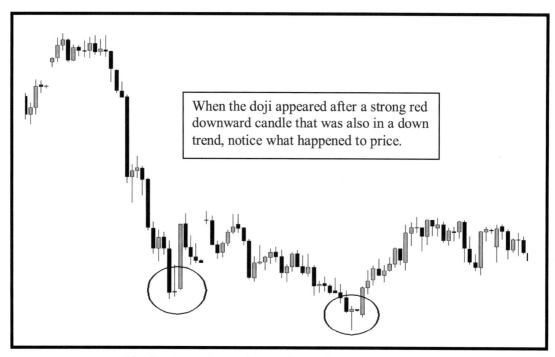

CS1.2 – Doji Examples at the End of a Downtrend

Below are some examples of the warning message of making a trade in the opposite direction of the trend based solely on the appearance of a doji. (See diagram **CS1.3**)

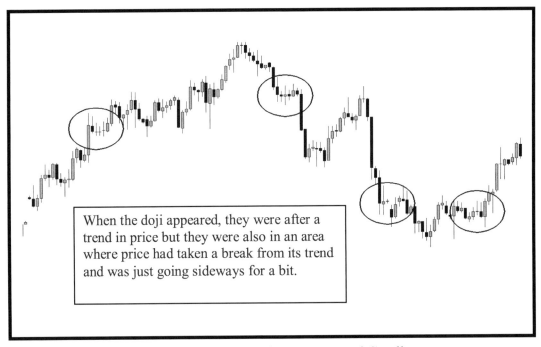

CS1.3 – Doji Examples as a Neutral Candle

When a doji is found where price is moving sideways it loses its significance and goes back to being neutral.

Summary: Although the doji by itself is a neutral candle, there are times when it is a *key* reversal indicator.

Spinning Tops
(Neutral or Reversal Candle)

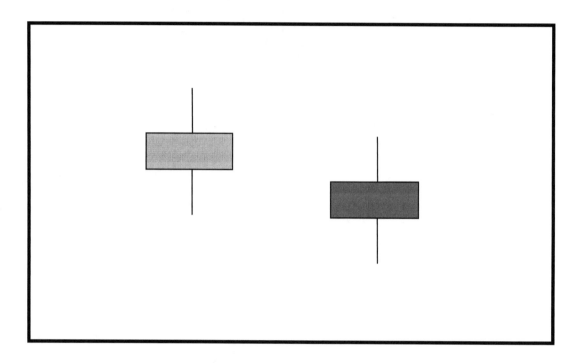

The spinning top is a very close relative of the Doji. They too show us that *neither* buyers nor sellers have had an advantage to move price significantly in their direction. They are basically telling us that the struggle between the buyers and sellers ended in a tie for the time frame of the chart we are looking at. If we were economists, we can say that the presence of spinning tops represents a relationship between supply and demand that is balanced.

The neutral status of the spinning top, like the doji, changes depending on the trend or candles that come before you see them on the chart. If a single spinning top or groups of spinning tops appear after a trend that is moving either up or down, then they start to take on significance.

Let's say that price has been trending down and there are several large red candles and then a group of spinning tops appears. In this scenario the sellers have had the advantage because supply has been greater than the current demand. Appearance of the spinning tops tells us that price, for the moment, has become balanced. Price may still continue in a downtrend, however, the spinning tops are a *warning* that price may now reverse and go the other way. (See diagram **CS1.4**)

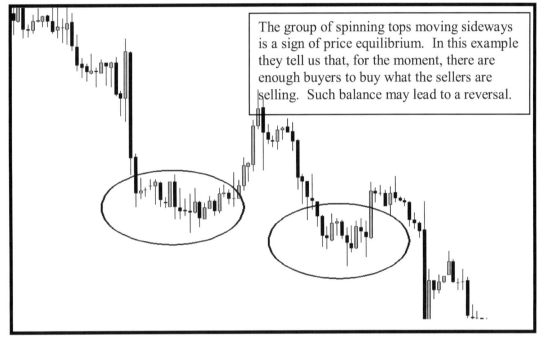

CS1.4 – Spinning Top Examples at the End of a Downtrend

Again, let's say that price has been trending up and there are several large green candles and then a group of spinning tops appears. In this scenario the buyers have had the advantage because demand has been greater than the available supply. The appearance of the spinning tops tell us that price, for the moment, has become balanced. Price may still continue in an uptrend, however, the spinning tops are a warning that price may now reverse and go the other way. (See diagram **CS1.5**)

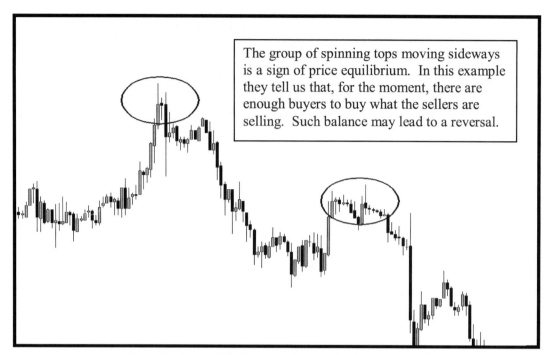

CS1.5 – Spinning Tops at the End of an Uptrend

Summary: Although spinning tops by themselves are neutral candles, there are times when they are a *key* reversal indicator.

3. Candlesticks
Spinning Tops

Refer to:
CD Disk 3

3.2. A Lesson in Spinning Tops (00:28)
Peter describes what a spinning top looks like.

3.3. Spinning Top Example (00:31)
An example of a spinning top at the end of an uptrend on the EUR/USD hourly chart causing a price reversal. The result was a fall in price to the tune of 70 pips.

The Hammer
(Reversal Candle)

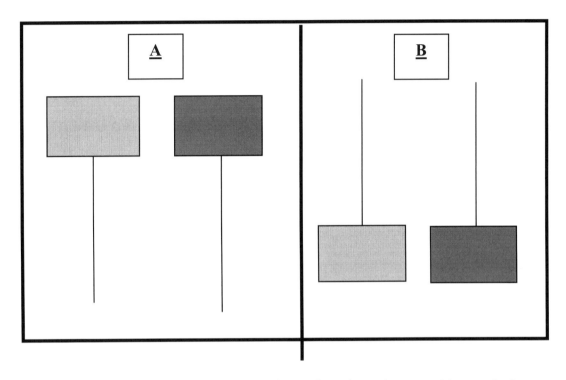

The Hammer is a *reversal* candlestick. They tell us that price was either pushed down or up to a certain level and that price level was *not* able to be sustained. The fact that the price level was not able to be sustained is indicative of a possible change in the direction will occur. To be a true hammer, the tail or wick needs to be at least *twice* as long as the body of the candle.

You would really like to see a hammer after a rally in price, like in diagram **CS1.6**. Even though price went sideways after the hammer, it was the basis for the eventual rally in the opposite direction. Price was not able to sustain lower prices, even though it tried to test the low of the first hammer, as can be seen by the hammer that occurred just before the rally up.

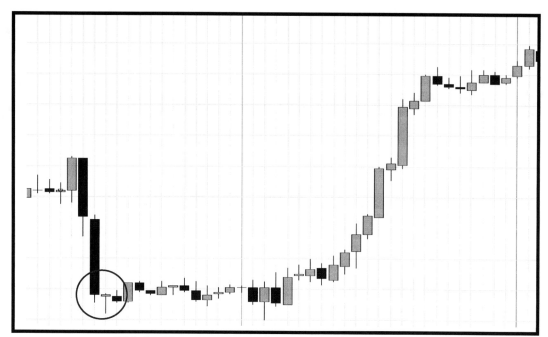

CS1.6 – Hammer Example at the End of a Downtrend

In diagram **CS1.7**, the hammer that has been noted was just after a large run up in price. The doji that preceded this hammer was a further indication that price was not able to sustain higher highs thus forcing price to retreat to lower levels.

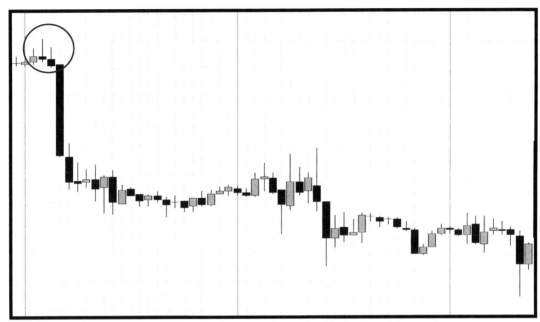

CS1.7 – Hammer Example at the End of an Uptrend

The hammer is what we refer to as an *exhaustion* indicator. Price is too tired to keep going in the direction it has been going and needs to take a break. What should you be thinking about doing if price was at M4 on an M2/M4 day and you see a hammer after the run up in price?

HAMMER CAUTION: You need to be careful of the hammers noted in diagram **CS1.8**. They are telling you that price could go either way and you are best to stand aside and wait until price decides which direction it would like to go. You do have some indication which way direction is going to go based on the appearance of the third hammer.

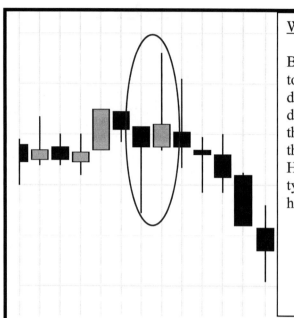

CS1.8 – Example of Back to Back Hammers

After you have gained some experience by observing the hammer in real time price action, they will no doubt start to become one of your *favorite* candles to show up; especially if they are high up in the sell region of the pivots or down low in buy region of the pivots.

3. Candlesticks
The Hammer

Refer to:
CD Disk 3

3.4. A Lesson in Hammers (01:57)
Peter describes what a hammer is and what it looks like.

3.5. Hammer Example 1 (00:30)
An example of a hammer at the end of an uptrend on the EUR/USD hourly chart causing a price reversal. The result was a fall in price to the tune of 70 pips.

3.6. Hammer Example 2 (00:21)
An example of a hammer at the end of a downtrend and an inverted hammer at the end of an uptrend.

3.7. Hammer Application in Trading (02:38)
Peter describes what a hammer is, where to look for hammers, and how to use hammers in conjunction with the other indicators taught in the course to make a trading decision.

3.8. Hammers Only Work at End of Run (01:17)
Hammers are only significant at the end of a nice uptrend or downtrend which eventually may lead to a price reversal.

3.9. Inverted Hammer Significance in a Downtrend (01:38)
With the help of another Forexmentor member, Peter answers a question submitted by a Forexmentor member in regards to the significant of inverted hammers in downtrends.

Bullish and Bearish Candlesticks
(Continuation Candles)

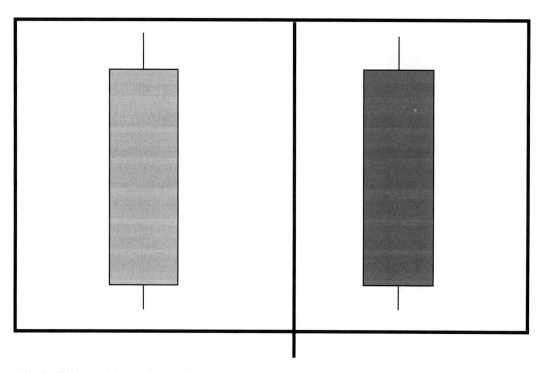

The bullish and bearish candlesticks are long strong looking candles. They usually have short tails and short wicks; they can even be seen *missing* a tail or a wick or both. The candles by themselves show you that price is moving *convincingly* up or down.

In diagram **CS1.9** you can see how the large green bullish candles were a significant sign that price was going to keep going up. Also note the large red bearish candle on the right side of the diagram. It was followed by a significant movement down in price.

CS1.9 – Examples of Bullish and Bearish Candles

When you see a bullish candle and bearish candle right next to each other, we call this candle pattern *railroad tracks*. After a rally up in price, we are anticipating that price will then go down. (See diagram **CS1.10**)

CS1.10 – Example of Railroad Tracks

Likewise, when we see a bearish candle and a bullish candle right next to each other after a rally down in price, we are anticipating that price will then go up.

Keep your eyes open for these bullish and bearish candles when they form railroad tracks. This pattern is telling you that the market has quickly changed its mind and wishes to go the opposite direction. Also, look for the candles on the break of a trendline or triangle pattern. You will learn about these a bit later, as they indicate the conviction of the direction price is going to move in.

3. Candlesticks
Railroad Tracks

Refer to:
CD Disk 3

3.10. A Lesson in Railroad Tracks 1 (00:45)
Peter explains what a railroad track is and clarifies the formation of a railroad track.

3.11. A Lesson in Railroad Tracks 2 (04:43)
Peter explains what a railroad track is and clarifies the formation of a railroad track. Peter also runs through some examples of railroad tracks on various currency pairs.

3.12. Railroad Tracks Example 1 (00:37)
An example of railroad tracks at the end of an uptrend.

3.13. Railroad Tracks Example 2 (00:27)
Examples of railroad tracks on the USD/JPY 15 minute chart.

3.14. Railroad Tracks Example 3 (00:36)
An example of railroad tracks at the end of a downtrend on the EUR/USD 5 minute chart.

3.15. Railroad Tracks Example 4 (00:12)
An example of railroad tracks at the end of a downtrend on the EUR/USD 5 minute chart.

3.16. Railroad Tracks Example 5 (00:57)
An example of railroad tracks at the end of a little uptrend in price on the EUR/USD 15 minute chart which lead to a fall in price to the tune of 20 pips.

3.17. Railroad Tracks Example 6 (01:09)
An example of railroad tracks at the end of an uptrend on the EUR/USD 5 minute chart.

3.18. Railroad Tracks Trading Example (01:53)
An example of railroad tracks at the end of an uptrend on the EUR/USD 5 minute chart which eventually lead to a price reversal and a fall in price. Profit for the day was 45 pips.

3.19. Railroad Tracks Size (01:05)
Two examples of railroad tracks on the EUR/USD 15 minute chart back to back. Peter warns you to not get hung up on the actual size of the candles but to focus on the formation of the railroad tracks.

3.20. Railroad Tracks Not Correctly Formed (01:02)
Peter corrects a submission from a Forexmentor member in regards to railroad tracks not correctly formed and the end of a downtrend.

Candlestick Charting

Personal Notes and Observations

Trendlines

Price moves in trends. The Forex market in particular is known for its strong price trends. Because of this, trendlines will prove to be a *powerful* technical tool to have in your technical toolbox. Although trendlines are one of the easier technical tools to understand, it can take some time and experimentation to know how to use them effectively. This is because trendlines represent *dynamic* support and resistance.

A good trendline is a representation of what the market is really doing with price. A trendline obviously shows you whether the market is moving price up or down. It also shows you the conviction of the current direction by the slope or steepness of the trendline. In addition, a trendline shows you the strength of the directional movement in price by the length of time it has been in place and the number of times price touches or approaches the trendline.

What do we mean when we say that trendlines are 'dynamic' points of support and resistance? Previously we have looked at support and resistance that is determined by historical price levels (see diagram **TL1.0**) or the mathematical calculations of pivot points. However, with trendlines there may be no actual previous price level providing support or resistance; price just seems to stop on the chart for no apparent reason and then go in the opposite direction. That is why trendlines are dynamic support and resistance because the support or resistance level they define *changes* with every tick of the chart.

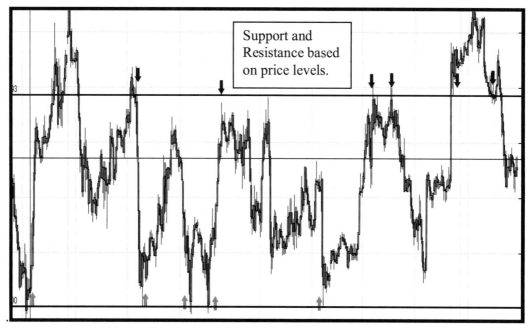

TL1.0 – Support and Resistance based on Price Levels

Notice how price moved along the trendlines we have drawn below. (See diagram **TL1.1**) The points of support and resistance defined by the trendlines were respected by price. It should be noted that some trendline support and resistance levels may line up with previous support or resistance levels generated by price but they do NOT have to.

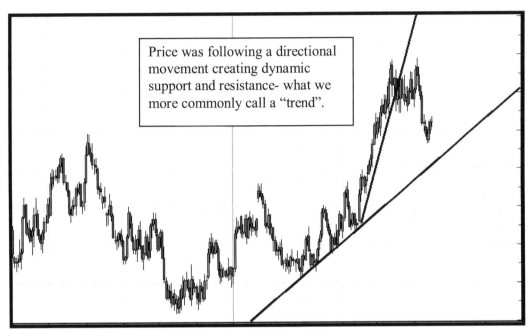

TL1.1 – Examples of Trendlines

We have broken the study of trendlines into two separate categories:

1. The common sense trendline
2. The Tom Demark trendline

Common Sense Trendlines

There are no rules to drawing common sense trendlines. When drawing trendlines in conjunction with candles, you will hear much discussion on the "right" way to draw common sense trendlines. The only criteria to note is that you should connect three or more peaks or troughs. You cannot draw a trendline with only one peak or trough. Well you can. It just won't have any significance.

Some people say that you should use the wicks of the candles to draw a trendline. (See diagram **TL1.2**)

TL1.2 – Common Sense Trendline Using Wicks of the Candles

Others will say that you need to use the bodies of the candles to draw your trendlines. (See diagram **TL1.3**)

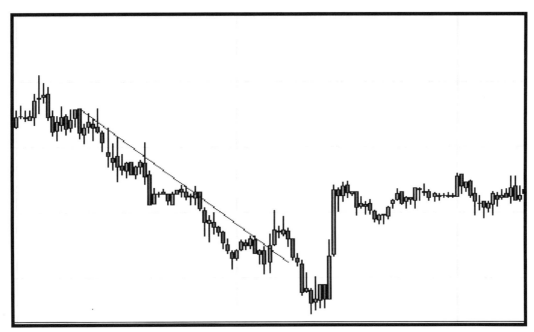

TL1.3 – Common Sense Trendline Using Bodies of the Candles

Which one of the two do you prefer? What you do not want to do is limit your technical analysis. This is what you could be doing if you begin to take sides in the arguments that surround the 'proper way to draw a common sense trendline'. You must remember that drawing trendlines is more a matter of common sense as opposed to using strict rules.

That being the case, I would like to submit the following recommendation. (See diagram **TL1.4**)

TL1.4 – Both Methods of Drawing Common Sense Trendlines

Use *both* the methods previously discussed together. What does this achieve? Primarily it keeps you out of pointless arguments. More importantly, it provides you with sound technical analysis. Trendline #1 shows the possible extremes price may go to while in this downtrend. While trendline #2 tracks the average point price will go to in this downtrend.

What does it mean when price breaks through a trendline? It could mean that price is going to start trending in the opposite direction. However, you should be using other indicators to help you make that analysis.

4. Trendlines
Common Sense Trendlines

Refer to:
CD Disk 4

4.1. Common Sense Trendlines Example 1 (03:40)
Peter shows us how his Peter Bain's Conceptual Line, also known as a common sense trendline, has held almost to the pip in the downtrend on the USD/CAD daily chart. As price comes up to test the common sense trendline, sell the rallies in the downtrend.

4.2. Common Sense Trendlines Example 2 (05:52)
Peter uses his Peter Bain's Conceptual Line, also known as a common sense trendline, on the EUR/USD hourly and 15 minute chart looking for and opportunity to buy the pair as price comes down to test/touch the PBCL in around the London close.

4.3. Common Sense Trendlines Trading Example 1 (02:24)
An example of a common sense trendline submitted by a Forexmentor member on the USD/CAD daily chart. As price comes up to test the trendline, sell the rallies in the downtrend in conjunction with using an oscillator indicator.

4.4. Common Sense Trendlines Trading Example 2 (01:54)
Multiple examples of common sense trendlines submitted by a Forexmentor member on the GBP/USD 15 minute chart.

Tom DeMark Trendlines

Now we come to the world of trendlines where there is NO argument on how to draw trendlines. The argument switches to whether or not these Tom DeMark trendlines are valid or true trendlines. As with the argument that surrounds how to draw trendlines discussed earlier, just stay out of it, and use this technical tool for your benefit.

The reason there is no argument on how to draw Tom Demark trendlines is because Tom DeMark invented the methodology, clearly defined it, and thus removed any element of subjectivity in drawing them by the technical analyst. So if you wish to argue about it, you will have to take it up with him. Since there is no argument associated with how to draw a Tom Demark trendline, you can discuss how price relates to these trendlines and everyone that knows how to draw them will see and know exactly what you are talking about.

Tom DeMark trendlines are *dynamic* in that you are always drawing a new trendline when the market tells you to.

A *swing high* is a candle on your chart with a top that is higher than the tops of the candles on either side of it. So you must have three COMPLETED candles in place to have a swing high. (See diagram **TL1.5** for examples of swing highs)

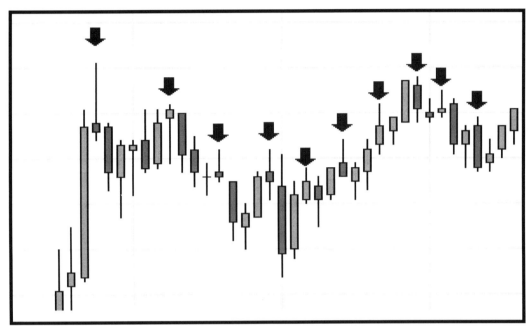

TL1.5 – Swing High Examples

Diagram **TL1.5** is from a very short time frame chart. You will not usually see this many swing highs this close together on a higher time frame chart. We used this example to emphasize what to look for.

A *swing low* is a candle on your chart with a bottom that is lower than the bottoms of the candles on either side of it. So you must have three COMPLETED candles in place to have a swing low. (See **TL1.6** for examples of swing lows)

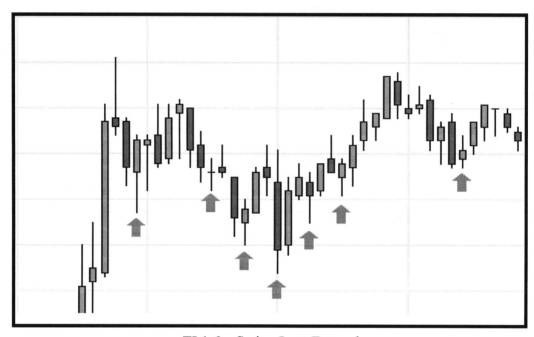

TL1.6 – Swing Low Examples

Again, diagram **TL1.6** is from a very short time frame chart. You will not usually see this many swing lows this close together on a higher time frame chart. We used this example to emphasize what to look for.

4. Trendlines
Swing Points

Refer to:
CD Disk 4

4.6. Determining Swing Points 1 (02:11)
Peter uses a conceptual diagram to explain various scenarios in determining swing points in order to construct TD trendlines.

4.7. Determining Swing Points 2 (01:44)
A swing point is still valid when there are candles literally only 1 pip above/below their neighboring candles on a supply/demand line.

4.8. Finding Swing Points (03:11)

Peter shows examples of swing points on the GBP/USD 15 minute chart. Also, Peter runs through an exercise of finding swing points.

Tom Demark *supply trendlines* are trendlines drawn to connect swing highs. You can also think of them as trendlines drawn on the topside of candles. Tom Demark supply trendlines are drawn by connecting the most recent swing high back to the previous swing high that is *higher* than the current swing high. Some people make the mistake of just connecting the most recent swing high to the swing high that occurred just prior to it, but this may not always be the correct swing high based on what was just described in the previous sentence. Now that you know what a swing high and a swing low looks like, let's use the same diagram to draw some examples of Tom Demark trendlines.

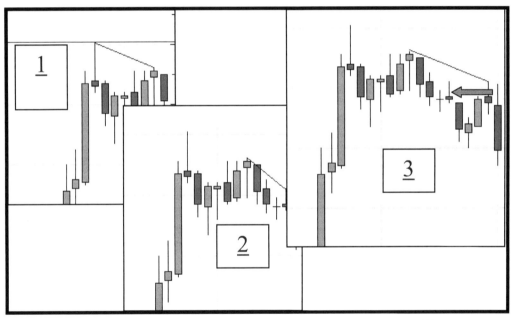

TL1.7 – Examples on How to Draw TD Supply Trendlines

The drawings numbered 1,2 and 3 in diagram **TL1.7** are examples of how you would connect the most recent Tom DeMark supply line in the order that they appeared in diagram **TL1.5**. Notice the swing high that the orange arrow is pointing to in diagram **TL1.7**. It would not be correct to draw the Tom DeMark supply trendline to that swing high because it is not *higher* than the most recent swing high. In diagram

How to Trade Currencies Like the 'Big Dogs'

TL1.7, the supply trendlines were not extended into the future but you *would* draw them extended into the future as shown in diagram **TL1.8**.

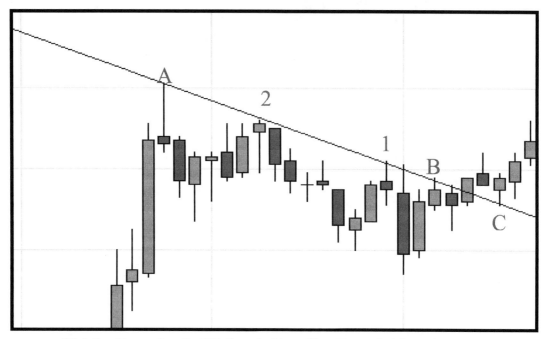

TL1.8 – Example of a TD Supply Trendline Extended into the Future

If the **#1** point occurred in real time and you connected the Tom Demark supply trendline back to the **#2** swing high with an extended trendline notice how well it tracked price back in history at point **A** and into the future at points **B** and **C**. When we extend our trendlines, we are able to see when price continues to use the trendline as resistance and also when price breaks through the resistance level the trendline is identifying to see if it will then turn into support as it did at point **C**.

You may be wondering what the real point behind these Tom DeMark trendlines is. They give an earlier indication that price may be starting to trend in a new direction and eventually penetrate a larger more significant common sense trendline, thus leading a larger change in price direction.

4. Trendlines
TD Supply Lines

Refer to:
CD Disk 4

4.9. Constructing TD Supply Lines (01:24)
Using a conceptual diagram, Peter shows you how to properly construct a TD supply line. Also, you want to get into the habit of extending your supply line out into the future and see how price action reacts in relation to the extension of the trendline

Tom Demark *demand trendlines* are trendlines drawn to connect swing lows. You can also think of them as trendlines drawn on the bottom of candles. Tom Demark demand trendlines are drawn by connecting the most recent swing low back to the previous swing low that is *lower* than the current swing low. Some people make the mistake of just connecting the most recent swing low to the swing low that occurred just prior to it, but this may not always be the correct swing low based on what was just described in the previous sentence. Now that you know what a swing high and a swing low looks like, let's use the same diagram to draw some examples of Tom Demark demand trendlines.

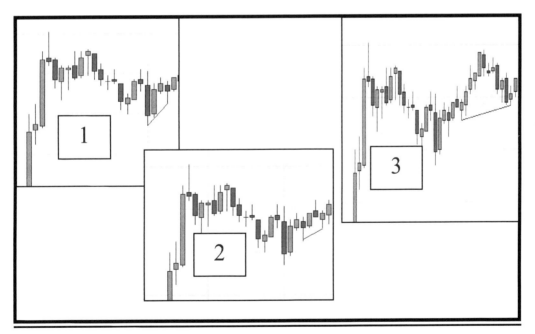

TL1.9 – Examples on How to Draw TD Demand Trendlines

The drawings numbered 1, 2 and 3 in diagram **TL1.9** are examples of how you would draw the most recent Tom DeMark demand lines in the order that they appeared in diagram **TL1.6**. As with the swing highs, it would not be correct to draw a Tom DeMark demand trendline to a swing low that is not *lower* than the most recent swing low. In diagram **TL1.9** the supply trendlines were not extended into the future but you *would* draw them extended into the future as shown in diagram **TL1.10**.

TL1.10 – Example of a TD Demand Trendline Extended into the Future

If the **#1** point occurred in real time and you connected the Tom Demark demand trendline back to the **#2** swing low with an extended trendline, notice how well it tracked price back in history and into the future. When we extend our trendlines, we are able to see when price continues to use the trendline as support and also when price breaks through the support level the trendline is identifying to see if it will then turn into resistance.

As you start working with common sense trendlines and Tom DeMark trendlines, you will begin to find how important they are to trading. The will become a significant tool in your trading toolbox of technical indicators.

Refer to:
CD Disk 4

4. Trendlines
TD Demand Lines

4.10. Constructing TD Demand Lines (01:40)
Using a conceptual diagram, Peter shows you how to properly construct a TD demand line. Also, you want to get into the habit of extending your demand line out into the future and see how price action reacts in relation to the extension of the trendline

Refer to:
CD Disk 4

4. Trendlines
TD Trendlines Examples

4.11. TD Trendlines Example 1 (01:18)
Examples of supply and demand trendlines on the EUR/USD 15 minute chart.

4.12. TD Trendlines Example 2 (05:44)
Examples of supply and demand trendlines on the EUR/USD 15 minute chart.

4.13. TD Trendlines Example 3 (06:10)
Examples of supply and demand trendlines on the EUR/USD hourly chart.

4.14. TD Trendlines Example 4 (01:21)
Examples of supply and demand trendlines on the EUR/USD 15 minute chart.

4.15. TD Trendlines Example 5 (02:07)
Examples of supply and demand trendlines on the EUR/USD 15 minute chart.

4.16. TD Trendlines Example 6 (00:46)
Examples of supply and demand trendlines on the EUR/USD 15 minute chart.

4.17. TD Trendlines Example 7 (00:34)
An example of a demand trendline on the EUR/USD 15 minute chart.

4.18. TD Trendlines Example 8 (01:11)

Examples of supply and demand trendlines on the EUR/USD daily chart.

4.19. TD Trendlines Example 9 (01:04)
An example of demand trendlines on the EUR/USD 15 and 5 minute chart.

4.20. TD Trendlines Example 10 (07:48)
Examples of supply and demand trendlines on the GBP/USD 15 minute chart.

4.21. TD Trendlines Example 11 (01:35)
Examples of supply and demand trendlines on the GBP/USD 15 minute chart.

4.22. TD Trendlines Drawing Example 1 (06:41)
How to construct supply and demand trendlines on the EUR/USD 15 minute chart and the application of the trendlines as price unfolds.

4.23. TD Trendlines Drawing Example 2 (06:17)
How to construct supply and demand trendlines on the GBP/USD 15 minute chart and the application of the trendlines as price unfolds.

4.24. TD Trendlines Drawing Example 3 (15:51)
How to construct supply and demand trendlines on the USD/JPY and GBP/USD 15 minute chart and the application of the trendlines as price unfolds.

4.25. TD Trendlines Drawing Example 4 (16:03)
How to construct supply and demand trendlines on the GBP/USD 15 minute chart and the application of the trendlines as price unfolds.

4.26. TD Trendlines Drawing Example 5 (17:38)
How to construct supply and demand trendlines on the USD/JPY 15 minute chart and the EUR/USD daily and 15 minute chart and the application of the trendlines as price unfolds.

4.27. TD Trendlines Drawing Example 6 (10:17)
How to construct supply and demand trendlines on the EUR/USD

15 minute chart and the application of the trendlines as price unfolds.

4.28. TD Trendlines Drawing Example 7 (10:47)
How to construct supply and demand trendlines on the EUR/USD 15 minute chart and the application of the trendlines as price unfolds.

4.29. TD Trendlines Drawing Example 8 (17:22)
How to construct supply and demand trendlines on the EUR/USD 15 minute chart and the application of the trendlines as price unfolds.

4.30. TD Trendlines Drawing Example 9 (07:34)
How to construct supply and demand trendlines on the EUR/USD 15 minute chart and the application of the trendlines as price unfolds.

4.31. TD Trendlines Drawing Example 10 (07:39)
How to construct supply and demand trendlines on the EUR/USD 15 minute chart and the application of the trendlines as price unfolds.

Trendlines

Personal Notes and Observations

MACD

In the next few sections we will be discussing indicators. I would just like to pause for a moment and have a discussion about what an indicator really is. Please indulge me. I think you will find it beneficial, if not today, maybe some day.

People throw around the word indicator as if its true meaning was some mathematical interpretation of price action that is supposed to be telling us where price is going or supposed to go. It is not uncommon to hear traders say things like, 'which indicator are you using?' or 'check out this indicator'. Before we get into whether or not those are beneficial ways of using the word 'indicator' in trading, let's do some analysis.

An indicator is a tool that interprets some sort of information and presents us with some meaningful value. It is a tool that communicates some sort of data to us. A speedometer is an indicator that measures the speed of a car, giving us a meaningful value so that we drive appropriately and do not receive a speeding ticket. Would a speedometer be useful to measure the temperature of a room? No, of course not. The speedometer is not built to measure temperature or generate a meaningful value to tell us how hot or cold it is. To effectively measure the temperature of a room you should use an indicator called a *thermostat*. This helps us to appreciate that using the wrong indicator to measure the wrong thing will not give you meaningful values for you to make important decisions. Just like a thermostat cannot show you how fast you are moving when the speed limit sign tells you to reduce your speed.

Indicators in trading must be approached in the same manner. You must use the right indicator to measure the right thing in order to make important trading decisions. That means you must know what your trading indicators are measuring and when they will and will not give you good information on which to base your trading decisions. I will tell you from experience that many traders use indicators but have no real idea how they function. Because of this, they make bad trading decisions that cost them real money. Had they taken the time to do their homework they would have saved themselves a lot of money. Take time to study each indicator you plan to use and back test it to make sure you have a good understanding of how it operates.

Indicators are mostly broken into two categories:

1. Trending indicators; these are "lagging" indicators, which means they follow price action.
2. Oscillating indicators; these are "leading" indicators, which means they anticipate where price will go.

The MACD is a trending indicator.

The MACD is perhaps one of the best known indicators; it is also one of the *most* misunderstood indicators. People tend to think of it as one indicator but it is not. It is a combination of three distinct components, two of which are separate indicators. The MACD acronym stands for Moving Average Convergence Divergence.

The three components are: (See diagram **MACD 1.0**)

1. The moving average crossovers
2. The histogram indicator
3. The neutral or center line

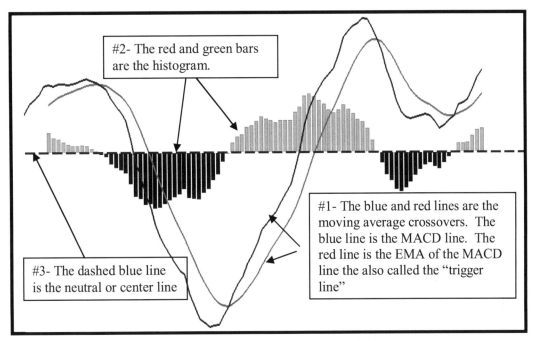

MACD1.0 – Three Components of MACD

Now that you know the names of the components, we need to tell you what those components are. The "fast line" also called the MACD line, represented in diagram **MACD1.0**, as the blue line, is the difference between the 26 EMA (Exponential Moving Average) of the *closing prices* subtracted from the 12 EMA of the *closing prices*. Remember this is a moving average directly based on *price*.

The "slow line" also called the trigger line, represented in diagram **MACD1.0**, by the red line, is a moving average of the *"fast line"* or *"MACD line"*. The "slow line" is calculated by taking the 9 EMA of the MACD line. It is sometimes called the moving average of the "fast line". Remember this is a moving average of the *MACD line*, not directly of price.

The MACD values 12, 26 and 9 will represent the time period being used on the chart you are viewing. On a daily chart they would represent the 12 day EMA, 26 day EMA and 9 day EMA (exponential moving averages). On a weekly chart they would represent the 12 week EMA, the 26 week EMA and the 9 week EMA (exponential moving averages). And so on for the specific time frame you are analyzing.

Take a moment to notice how the lines (exponential moving averages) cross each other in diagram **MACD1.1** (we have changed the colors on the MACD here to show how it can be helpful for you to have the colors changed to be both green for going up and both red for going down). This crossing of the lines usually indicates that the current uptrend or current downtrend has completed its run and is now reversing direction (notice I said "usually"; we will look at the exception to this later on under the subject of divergence).

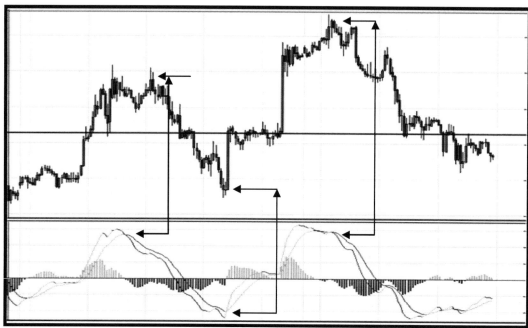

MACD1.1 – MACD Lines Crossing Examples

The next part of the MACD indicator we will discuss is the *histogram*. The histogram is the vertical bar formations, colored green and red, that appear above and below the neutral line in diagram **MACD1.2**. It represents the difference between

MACD and the 9-day EMA of MACD. The histogram was developed to give an earlier indication that the MACD lines were getting ready to cross. The histogram is actually an indicator *of the MACD*. That is why it is usually best to compare the histogram to the moving average lines first instead of directly to price. Do not worry if you are having a little difficulty getting your brain around this, we will be going through some examples shortly.

When the histogram crosses over the center line, it *correlates exactly* to the MACD line crossing over the trigger line. When the MACD line, (the blue line in **MACD1.2**) is above the trigger line (the red line in **MACD1.2**), the histogram will be on the top of the centerline. However, if the MACD line is below the trigger line, the histogram will be below the neutral line.

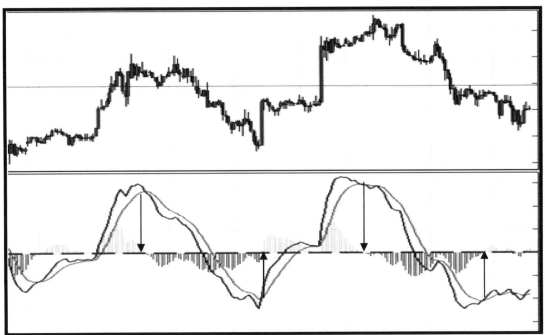

MACD1.2 – Histogram Correlating with MACD Lines Crossing

The histogram can also be used as a visible representation of the power, force or momentum of price movement. Notice the length of the histogram bars in relation to the movement made by price in diagram **MACD1.3**.

Let's take a moment to consider this idea of momentum, power and force. While this subject will be fairly easy to convey to you, it is usually difficult for people to remember when they are trading, so please try to keep this subject in mind as you begin and continue to trade.

Imagine that you have just thrown a ball into the air. When the ball first leaves your hand, its velocity, force and momentum are *very* rapid and forceful. However, as the ball rises, it gradually loses its momentum and force to keep moving up. At its peak, the ball has a moment of equilibrium where it is not going any higher *nor* is it moving any lower. Gradually it begins to fall back to the ground. The histogram attempts to tell us *when* that point of equilibrium in price occurs before the MACD lines actually show us that the trend is changing.

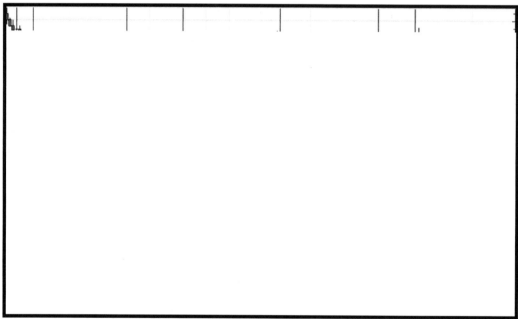

MACD1.3 – Histogram Point of Equilibrium in Price Examples

5. MACD
MACD Indicator

Refer to:
CD Disk 5

5.1. MACD Histogram Examples (06:19)
Examples between the relationship of the MACD moving average lines crossing and the MACD histogram at the neutral line submitted by a Forexmentor member. Also, further analysis in regards to the shift in momentum on the histogram can signal a pending price reversal.

The final part of the MACD indicator we will examine is the *center* or *neutral line*. It may appear to just be a line that identifies the upper and lower regions of the MACD.

However, there has been a lot written about how the centerline of the MACD is the key to the power of the indicator. I refer to the center line as the "teller of truth". It is easy for underwater divers to get disoriented if they are in an underwater cavern or diving at night. They can actually lose their sense of direction, not knowing where the surface of the water is. To correct their orientation between up and down, the divers can simple release some air bubbles and follow them up to the surface of the water. When you are trading in the market, it is easy to get disoriented in regards to the direction of the trend. Like the simple reorientation exercise of the diver, the trader simply needs to look at the center line of the MACD indicator. When the moving average lines are above the neutral line, the trend is up and when the moving average lines are below the neutral line the trend is down. If you need to get your bearings on the truth about the direction of the trend, use the center line as your point of reference. (See diagram **MACD1.4**)

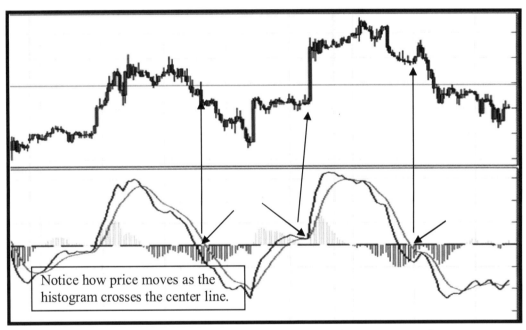

MACD1.4 – Neutral Line Point of Reference Examples

5. MACD
MACD Indicator

Refer to:
CD Disk 5

5.2. MACD Neutral Line (01:19)
Considerations when determining the trend above/below the neutral line.

MACD Neutralization and Divergence

Remember when we said that there will be an exception to when the MACD follows price? This is where we will discuss that exception. Please look at diagram **MACD1.5**. Notice how price is going up or staying the same and the MACD crossovers are going down. This separation from its normal function of following price is called DIVERGENCE. Because the MACD is NOT following price, it is warning us that there is some underlying weakness in the price and that it is *likely* to fall.

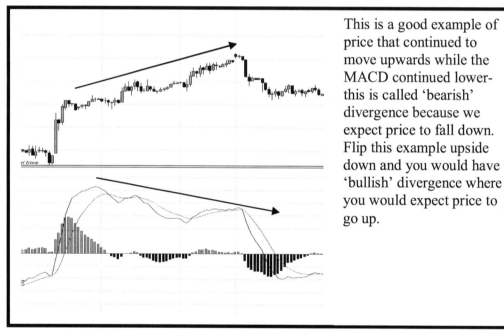

This is a good example of price that continued to move upwards while the MACD continued lower- this is called 'bearish' divergence because we expect price to fall down. Flip this example upside down and you would have 'bullish' divergence where you would expect price to go up.

MACD1.5 – Negative (Bearish) Divergence Example

Many traders see divergence and automatically think that it is going to play out into a *big* price move in the opposite direction that price has recently been trending in. Remember, trading the markets is a probability game. There are NO "for sures" or "guarantees", only probabilities.

5. MACD
MACD Neutralization and Divergence

Refer to:
CD Disk 5

5.3. How Reliable is Divergence (00:33)
No guarantees on how far price will reverse when divergence occurs.

When you see MACD divergence, one of TWO things will happen: 1) price will move in the opposite direction it has been moving in respective to the time frame it appears in and (divergence will play out) or 2) MACD will neutralize. Let's discuss these two items.

1. MACD divergence will show up in every time frame at one time or another. Please remember that the larger the time frame that any technical indicator appears in the more *significant* it becomes. For example, MACD divergence on the 5 minute chart may only cause price to move 5-10 pips, on the 15 minute chart 10-30 pips, on the 60 minute chart 30-80 pips and on the 4 hour chart 70-150 pips. Those values are not rules stamped in stone; they are more of a guide so that you have the proper expectation of price movement respective to the time frame you see the MACD divergence in.

5. MACD
MACD Divergence

Refer to:
CD Disk 5

5.4. MACD Divergence Examples (10:02)
Three example of positive and negative divergence back to back on the GBP/USD hourly chart.

5.5. MACD Negative Divergence Example 1 (02:22)
An example of negative divergence, also known as 'bearish' divergence, on the EUR/USD daily chart.

5.6. MACD Negative Divergence Example 2 (04:44)
An example of negative divergence, also known as 'bearish' divergence, on the USD/CAD monthly chart.

5.7. MACD Negative Divergence Example 3 (00:47)
An example of negative divergence, also known as 'bearish' divergence, on the EUR/USD daily chart.

5.8. MACD Negative Divergence Example 4 (03:22)
An example of negative divergence, also known as 'bearish' divergence, on the EUR/USD 15 and 5 minute chart.

5.9. MACD Negative Divergence Example 5 (01:58)
An example of negative divergence also known as 'bearish' divergence, on the EUR/USD hourly and 15 minute chart.

5.10. MACD Negative Divergence Example 6 (02:25)
An example of negative divergence, also known as 'bearish' divergence, on the EUR/USD monthly chart.

5.11. MACD Negative Divergence Example 7 (02:53)
Examples of negative divergence, also known as 'bearish' divergence, on the EUR/USD hourly and 15 minute chart.

5.12. MACD Negative Divergence Example 8 (00:53)
Three examples of negative divergence, also known as 'bearish' divergence, on the EUR/USD daily and 15 minute chart.

5.13. MACD Positive Divergence Example 1 (01:13)
An example of positive divergence, also known as 'bullish' divergence, on the EUR/USD 15 minute chart.

5.14. MACD Positive Divergence Example 2 (00:24)
An example of positive divergence, also known as 'bullish' divergence, on the EUR/USD 15 minute chart.

5.15. MACD Positive Divergence Example 3 (00:43)
An example of positive divergence, also known as 'bullish' divergence, on the EUR/USD 15 minute chart.

5.16. MACD Positive Divergence Example 4 (01:53)
An example of positive divergence, also known as 'bullish' divergence, on the EUR/USD 15 minute chart.

5.17. Importance of Divergence in Higher Timeframes (00:32)
Divergence on a higher timeframe generally has a greater impact, more price movement, longer lasting effect and a more powerful indication of a price trend reversal. Please note, this isn't a rule cast in stone, just a general guideline.

2. There will be times when you see MACD divergence appear on a price chart and as the MACD comes near to or crosses the center line there is NO significant price movement in the opposite direction that price has been moving. The MACD and price then again start to move together in the direction that price was moving. Because the divergence does not generate a price move in the opposite direction, a price reversal, the MACD divergence is then considered to be neutralized at that point and MACD should go back to its normal job of following price. (See diagram **MACD1.6**)

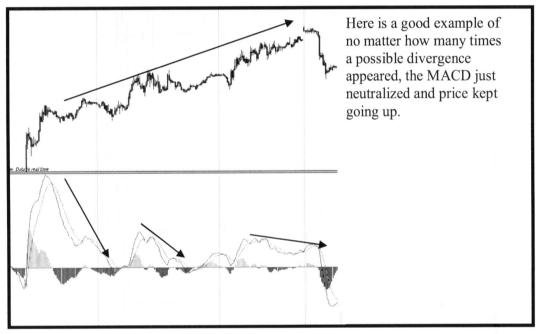

MACD1.6 – Neutralization Example

5. MACD
MACD Neutralization

Refer to:
CD Disk 5

5.18. MACD Neutralization Explained 1 (15:05)
Peter explains the concept of neutralization on the EUR/USD hourly and 15 minute chart.

5.19. MACD Neutralization Explained 2 (05:52)
Peter explains the concept of neutralization on the EUR/USD hourly and 15 minute chart. Peter also explains the difference

between divergence and neutralization.

5.20. MACD Neutralization Explained 3 (03:56)
Peter explains the concept of neutralization on the EUR/USD hourly and 15 minute chart. Peter also explains the difference between divergence and neutralization.

5.21. MACD Neutralization Explained 4 (05:14)
Peter explains the concept of neutralization on the EUR/USD hourly and 15 minute chart.

5.22. MACD Neutralization or Divergence (01:45)
Peter explains the difference between neutralization and divergence on the EUR/USD 15 minute chart.

5.23. MACD Neutralization Example 1 (01:36)
An example of neutralization in a downtrend on the EUR/USD hourly and 15 minute chart. Peter also explains the difference between divergence and neutralization.

5.24. MACD Neutralization Example 2 (01:33)
An example of neutralization in a downtrend on the GBP/USD 15 minute chart. Peter also explains the difference between divergence and neutralization.

5.25. MACD Neutralization Example 3 (01:26)
An example of neutralization in a downtrend on the USD/CAD 15 minute chart.

5.26. MACD Neutralization Example 4 (01:19)
An example of neutralization in an uptrend on the EUR/USD hourly chart.

5.27. MACD Neutralization Example 5 (03:21)
Three examples of neutralization submitted by a Forexmentor member on the EUR/USD 15 minute chart.

The MACD indicator is a wonderful and powerful tool to have in your toolbox of technical indicators. It may take a bit of time to understand how the different pieces of it work together and how to identify divergence and neutralization—but when you do, oh how powerful this indicator can be.

MACD

Personal Notes and Observations

Stochastics

George Lane developed the stochastic indicator. It is a *leading* indicator that can help in timing the points where price may reverse. The formula for the indicator is based on the premise that prices in a recent uptrend close near their highs and prices in a recent downtrend close near their lows. If price continues to move higher overall but the closing prices of the candles you are watching start to not close near their highs, the stochastic indicator will visually suggest to you that a reversal or pull back in price is imminent. (See diagram **ST1.0**)

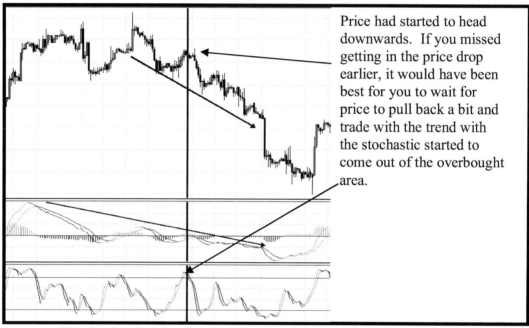

Price had started to head downwards. If you missed getting in the price drop earlier, it would have been best for you to wait for price to pull back a bit and trade with the trend with the stochastic started to come out of the overbought area.

ST1.0 – Stochastics Overbought Suggesting a Possible Fall in Price

You must remember when trading with the stochastic indicator that you should NOT jump right into a trade going the opposite way when the %D and the %K lines head into the overbought or oversold range which is identified by the horizontal bars in diagram **ST1.1**.

Pay close attention to the vertical blue line. As the stochastic indicator hit the oversold area price continued to drop quite a bit more. You should always wait until the stochastic indicator has some curl back up and is coming out of the oversold area before entering a trade. NEVER jump into a trade going against price when the stochastic indicator is just entering either the oversold or the overbought area.

ST1.1 – Entering a Trade Too Early with Stochastics

It is usually best to wait for the stochastic to come out of the overbought (reading of 80 and above) or out of the oversold (reading of 20 and below). The reason for that is that as you start to work with the stochastic indicator you will see there are times when it will stay in the overbought or oversold area for quite a long time. When the stochastic is staying in an overbought or oversold region for a long period of time, it is simply indicating that the current price trend is strong. (See diagram **ST1.2**)

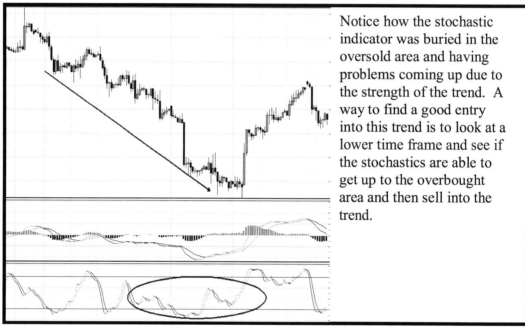

ST1.2 – Stochastics Remaining Oversold Over a Period Time

The stochastic indicator can be a great help in timing the entries to your trades and assist you when you are trying to trade with the trend. Make sure you get some experience with it and watch out for those times when the stochastic indicator 'gets stuck' in the oversold or overbought area because the trend is very strong.

6. Stochastics
Stochastics Indicator

Refer to:
CD Disk 6

6.1. Trading With Stochastics (07:01)
Using the USD/CAD daily chart, Peter shows you how to use stochastics and TD trendlines to time buy & sell entries buying the dips in an uptrend and selling the rallies in a downtrend.

6.2. Using Stochastics (02:05)
An example of the EUR/USD with stochastics plotted on the 15 & 5 minute chart looking for oversold conditions on stochastics buying the dips in an uptrend.

6.3. Buying the Dips in an Uptrend with Stochastics (00:33)
Another example of the EUR/USD with stochastics plotted on the 5 minute chart looking for oversold conditions on stochastics buying the dips in an uptrend.

6.4. Trading into a Trend Using Stochastics and MACD (03:06)
Peter explains how to trade the ensuing uptrend on the EUR/USD 15 minute chart buying the dips in an uptrend using stochastics and MACD on the 5 minute chart.

Stochastics

Personal Notes and Observations

Price Projections

Price projections are used to give a trader and idea of how far price will move in a certain direction. This can help a trader in determining where to exit a profitable trade. We will look at three different price projection methodologies:

- Average Daily Range Price Projections
- Triangle Price Projections
- Head and Shoulders Price Projections

Average Daily Range Price Projection

The Average Daily Range is a numerically calculated value obtained by taking a period of time, like that last month, and taking the total number of pips the currency pair moved during the month and dividing it by the number of days you used to come up with the total number of pips. Please do not confuse this with the technical indicator that is also named average daily range.

Let's assume that the Average Daily Range is 74 pips for the EURUSD. If you were to get into a trade going short the EUR at 1.2580 you could anticipate that price should move its average daily range in the direction of your trade reaching a price of 1.2506 at some time during the trading day.

Refer to:
CD Disk 6

7. Price Projections
<u>Average Daily Range Price Projections</u>

7.1. Determining the Average Daily Range (01:54)
Peter explains how the average daily range is determined and also comments on the ADR for holidays.

7.2. Average Daily Range Explained (02:26)
Once again, Peter explains how the average daily range is calculated, which is also known as the Actual Range in the Pivot Calculator on the Forexmentor members website. The projected range is also clarified.

7.3. Average Daily Range 24 Hours (00:25)
Peter explains the ADR applies for the fully 24 hours period, from midnight to midnight.

7.4. Average Daily Range Data 1 (00:35)

The average daily range figures for the major currency pairs.

7.5. Average Daily Range Data 2 (00:48)
The average daily range figures for the major currency pairs and the Aussie Dollar.

7.6. Average Daily Range for Various Currency Pairs (00:35)
The average daily range for various currency pairs was calculated by a Forexmentor member using historical data ranging from 2 to 4 years. An excel spreadsheet with the ADR calculations is available for download on the Forexmentor website.

7.7. Average Daily Range Analysis (01:32)
Courtesy FX Engines, the four major pairs average daily range in pips are broken down into hours of the day, trading session, days of the week, and days of the month.

7.8. Average Daily Range Clarified (03:08)
Peter warns to not get hung up on just the 76 pip average daily range projection for the EUR/USD but to use proper technical analysis when making a trading decision.

7.9. Average Daily Range Varies Day to Day (01:17)
The 76 pip ADR paradigm for the EUR/USD does not always play out the same everyday.

7.10. Average Daily Range for EURUSD (01:59)
With the EUR/USD having a minimum ADR of 76 pips, there is no reason why one could not easily carve out just 20 to 30 pips a day out of the 76 pips available.

Triangle Price Projection

There are two ways to do a price projection out of a triangle: one is based on price movement and the other is based on time.

To complete a triangle price projection based on price you:
1. Draw a vertical line from across the widest part of the triangle.
2. Copy the vertical line and paste it at the point where price breaks out of the triangle. This should give you the distance price may run once it breaks out of the triangle. (See diagram **PRIPRO1.0**)

PRIPRO1.0 – Triangle Price Projection Example Based on Price Movement

To complete a triangle price projection based on time, first you draw your trendlines to create the triangle and then you draw a vertical line at the triangles apex, the point at which the two trendlines intersect. When price reaches the vertical line that you have drawn through the apex, it will be close to the end of its run (maximum profit from the breakout of the triangle) and either getting ready to continue its trend or reverse. (See diagram **PRIPRO1.1**)

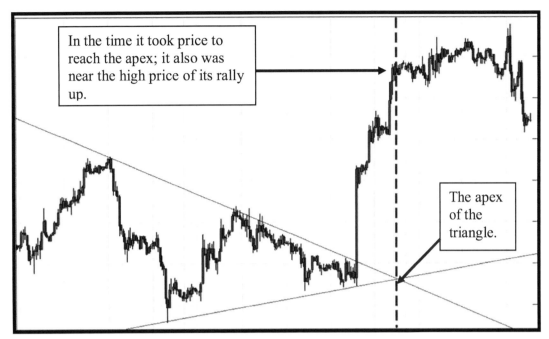

PRIPRO1.1 – Triangle Price Projection Example Based on Time

Refer to:
CD Disk 6

7. Price Projections
Triangle Price Projections

7.11. Triangle Price Projection 1 (01:13)
An example of a triangle price projection based on price fulfilled on the GBP/USD hourly chart.

7.12. Triangle Price Projection 2 (01:51)
Examples of a triangle price projections based on time fulfilled on the EUR/USD on multiple time frames.

7.13. Triangle Price Projection 3 (02:01)
Another example of a triangle price projection based on time fulfilled on the EUR/USD hourly chart.

Head and Shoulders Price Projection

After you have identified either a head and shoulders or an inverted head and shoulders complete the following steps:

1. Draw the neckline.
2. Measure the distance in pips from the head directly to the neckline.
3. Take the pip measurement that you just calculated and add it to where price completed the head and shoulders pattern by breaking through the neckline.

The time that it takes for price to reach head and shoulders price projection value you have come up with can take some time to reach. You can expect price to move up and down before it reaches its destination. (See diagram **PRIPRO1.2**)

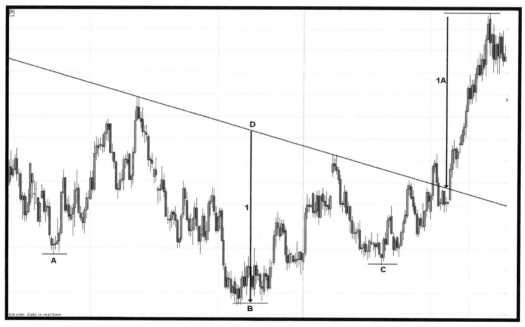

PRIPRO1.2 – Inverted Head and Shoulders Price Projection Example

The head and shoulders price projection method works for both regular head and shoulders patterns and inverted head and shoulders patterns as seen in diagram **PRIPRO1.2**.

We have only presented a couple of price projection methods that traders use; there are several. Experiment with these and be prepared to add others to you technical toolbox as you develop as a trader.

7. Price Projections
Head and Shoulders Price Projections

Refer to:
CD Disk 6

7.14. Head and Shoulders Price Projection 1 (02:51)
An example of a head and shoulders price projection fulfilled on the EUR/USD hourly chart.

7.15. Head and Shoulders Price Projection 2 (05:11)
An example of a head and shoulders price projection fulfilled on the GBP/USD 4 hour chart.

7.16. Inverted Head and Shoulders Price Projection (05:42)
An example of an inverted head and shoulders price projection on the GBP/USD weekly chart

Price Projections

Personal Notes and Observations

Time of Day

It is crucial to your trading that you are aware of some specific times of day from around the world. The reason for this is that the Forex market is traded worldwide and can be impacted by the opening of any of the major financial markets around the world. (All times EDT)

Time	Days	Event
7 pm	Sun – Thurs	Tokyo Market Opens
8 pm	Sun - Thurs	
9 pm	Sun – Thurs	Singapore and Hong Kong Markets Open
10 pm	Sun – Thurs	
11 pm	Sun – Thurs	
Midnight	Sun – Thurs	
1 am	Mon – Fri	
2 am	Mon – Fri	Frankfurt Market Opens
3 am	Mon – Fri	London Market Opens
4 am	Mon – Fri	Asia Markets Closing
5 am	Mon – Fri	
6 am	Mon – Fri	
7 am	Mon – Fri	
8 am	Mon – Fri	US Bond Markets Open/Most US News is 8:30am
9 am	Mon – Fri	9:30 USA New York Markets Open
10 am	Mon – Fri	Frankfurt Market Closing
11 am	Mon – Fri	London Market Closing
Noon	Mon – Fri	
1 pm	Mon – Fri	
2 pm	Mon – Fri	
3 pm	Mon – Fri	
4 pm	Mon – Fri	
5 pm	Mon – Fri	Australia Markets Open
6 pm	Mon - Fri	

TOD1.0 – Approximate Times for World Markets

Table **TOD1.0** is an approximate list of the times when most of the major world markets open for trading. It is also important to know that different countries change for daylight savings time on different dates, or if they even use daylight savings time at all. From time to time during the year check www.timeanddate.com to verify what the time difference is for the major world markets in comparison to New York Eastern Time. You can also check the various Forex news sites on the internet as they usually alert traders when a time change is going to occur for a particular world market. Additionally, there are a variety of time clocks you can add to your computer to instantly show you what time it is in any part of the world. You will find suggestions for these clocks in the *Getting Started* video in the AM Review.

Refer to:
CD Disk 6

8. Time of Day
<u>Time of Day</u>

8.1. Forex Hours of Operation by Location 1 (01:56)
A chart submitted by a Forexmentor member indicating the Forex hours of operation in EST for all major locations with also the line graph for the daily trading volume for the Forex overlaid on top.

8.2. Forex Hours of Operation by Location 2 (01:56)
This video shows how the Forex hours of operation chart evolved into the current version from two previous sources submitted separately by two other Forexmentor members.

8.3. Times of the Day Chart (02:03)
A chart created by a Forexmentor member that shows the open and close times for the major markets around the world.

8.4. GMT Times of the Markets (00:46)
A table created by a Forexmentor member displays all the major markets open and close times in various time zones including GMT time.

8.5. Time and Date Link (00:43)
Here is the link to the website Time and Date. One handy tool called the Time Zone Converter allows you to specify a date and time at one location, and it will convert it to other zones you request.

8.6. World Market Hours Link (00:55)
The website World Market Hours offers market opening and closing times, counts down to the open and close of different markets, and also provides a conversion tool from GMT Time to your local time.

8.7. Time Zone Conversion (00:27)
A time zone conversion table.

8.8. Daylight Savings (01:07)
Information on daylight savings for various time zones.

8. Time of Day
Clocks

Refer to:
CD Disk 6

8.9. A Members FX Market Time Program (00:54)
A Forex market time zone program available for download in the Forexmentor member's area which adjusts automatically for daylight savings around the world.

8.10. SymmTime Clock (00:17)
A screenshot of the SymmTime clock program and also the download link for the program.

8.11. ZoneTick Clock (00:29)
The download link for the ZoneTick World Time Zone Clock.

8.12. Clock Software (00:29)
Information on two different free desktop clocks.

8.13. Clocks, Clocks, and More Clocks (02:47)
Information on various free desktop clocks, websites with time zone converters and tips on configuring your PC for daylight savings.

Again, price has a *tendency* to start moving in and around the opening of the major financial markets of the world. In particular, you should pay attention to the London open, the New York open and the London close. Price action can continue to move in the direction it has been trending with even more momentum, or quickly reverse and go the other way. So be aware of the time at which those markets open and close.

Refer to:
CD Disk 6

8. Time of Day
Specific Times of Day

8.14. Times of the Day to Watch Out For (00:29)
Peter lists various times of the day that you should be aware of. For example, in around the London open, more times then not price will either continue in the current trend with more momentum or quickly reverse.

8.15. Important Trading Times (01:11)
Peter talks about times of the day that you should watch out for. Stuff does happen at these times.

8.16. Reversal at the London Open (00:31)
An example on the EUR/USD 15 minute chart of a reversal in around the London Open.

8.17. Pay Attention to Certain Times for Trading Opportunities (00:44)
Peter uses the EUR/USD 15 minute chart and shows 3 examples of trading opportunities at specific times of the day.

8.18. Grabbing 20 Pips at the London Close (00:32)
The London Close more often then not can be a good opportunity to carve out 20 pips.

8.19. A Caution on Open and Close Times 1 (01:52)
Peter reiterates that stuff doesn't always happen exactly at a certain time. For example, price doesn't necessary always reverse exactly at the London Open at 3:00am EST.

8.20. A Caution on Open and Close Times 2 (03:05)
Peter reiterates that stuff doesn't always happen exactly at a certain time. For example, price doesn't necessary always reverse exactly at the London Open at 3:00am EST.

The global trading sessions basically can be divided up the following way:

- Asia (also called Tokyo session): 7pm-4am Eastern Time
- European (also called London session): 3am-11:30am Eastern Time
- US (also called the New York session): 8am-5pm Eastern Time

The following are key times to watch as there could be large moves associated with the large volume of transactions occurring:

- Asian-European Overlay: 2am-4am Eastern Time
- European-Us Overlay: 8am-11:30am Eastern Time

A key reason to be aware of when the sessions switch is that the market direction could switch too.

Refer to:
CD Disk 6

8. Time of Day
Trading Sessions

8.21. Forex Daily Trading Activity (00:37)
A line graph submitted by a Forexmentor member that shows the daily trading volume for the Forex.

8.22. Non-London Trading Hours (01:01)
Though Peter focuses mostly on the London session, there are certainly trading opportunities in other trading sessions such as the Asian session. For example, you can choose to trade the USD/JPY pair which occupies most of the volume during the Asian session.

8.23. Asian Hour Trading (00:38)
A Forexmentor member shares his success on a specific trade he made on the GBP/USD during the Asian session. At times the Asian session can be anemic however in this case, there was significant movement.

8.24. What Time to Start Trading (01:26)
When considering a position during the London Session, between 2 to 4am EST will generally yield a good trading opportunity. Stuff doesn't always happen exactly at a certain time. This business is about probabilities, something will probably happen, but no guarantees.

Time of Day

Personal Notes and Observations

Commitment of Traders (COT)

The Commitments of Traders report (COT) can be a very useful tool in trading the Forex markets if they are used correctly and carefully. The United States CFTC keeps records of positions taken by traders in the commodity futures market. Even though the commodity Forex futures market is not the same as the Spot Forex market, it can give us advanced notice that trends in the Forex market could be changing.

The CFTC produces a weekly report that shows the number of long or short contracts held by the all important commercial traders, large investors and smaller ones (like you and me). This report is generated weekly and is available for free for everyone in the world to see.

What is the significance of this? Well suppose that Warren Buffet called you up and said tomorrow I am going to buy 2 million shares of the Gap company, what would you think was the smart thing to do? Since he is one of the biggest dogs out there, the smart thing to do would be to buy Gap stock. This is the principle behind trading with the COT data.

The CFTC produces a very large and complicated numerical report, which can be found at: http://cftc.gov/cftc/cftccotreports.htm. It could take a person weeks or months of studying to be able to grasp how to interpret all of this data. Fortunately for us, Barry Lees has developed a way to interpret this data graphically. You can access Barry's graphical representation of this data at the following website: http://www.cot-futures.com/cot/index.htm.

At Barry's site, you can access week old data for free. You can also pay a small yearly subscription fee to Barry to have access to the real time data that is released late Friday afternoons Eastern Time USA; well worth the small yearly fee Barry asks in return for his graphical representation. Let's take a look at how to use the COT data as Barry presents it. (See diagram **COT1.0**. Please refer to video tutorials for proper color representations.)

Notice in the diagram that after the Commercial traders were very short the EUR based on seeing the orange line all the way at the bottom the EURUSD price chart showed the EUR getting much weaker and the Commercial traders unloaded their Euros in the market. (See diagram **COT1.1**)

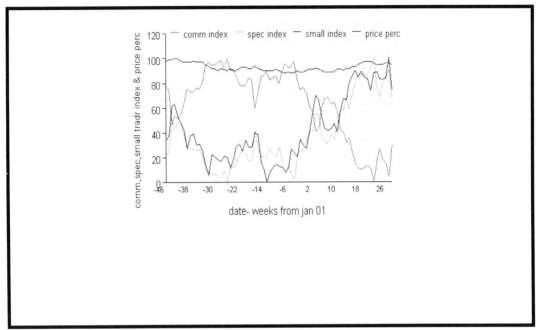

COT1.0 – Commercial Traders Extremely Short EURUSD

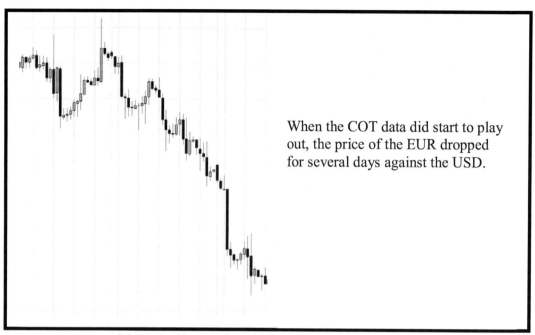

COT1.1 – Dramatic Fall in Price on the EURUSD

Here is the caution related to the COT data reports. You cannot trade this data just by *itself*. It is just like any other technical indicator that you use. You must use several indicators working together creating a *confluence* of events leading to a trade with high probability of profits. This data can take anywhere from three weeks to three months to play out. Please keep that in mind when you are using the COT data to trade.

9. Commitment of Traders (COT)
COT Part I

Refer to:
CD Disk 7

9.1. COT Website Introduction (02:09)
The link to the COT website is shown. You have a choice of paying a small monthly fee of $4.95 US, to become a member and have access to real-time data or you can choose the visitor option, which is free, but the data is delayed by one week. The main report page with the list of commodities including currencies you see when you log in either as a member or visitor is shown in this video.

9.2. Main Report Page Explanation (08:52)
Definitions for each of the columns on the main report page are explained. The columns discussed are 'Commodity', 'Exchange', 'Net-Ndx Comm', 'Net-Ndx Spec', and 'Span'.

9.3. Euro FX Report Introduction (01:48)
The Euro FX will be used as our example. The main page for the Euro FX report is shown which contains 78 weeks of COT data.

9.4. Finding the Euro FX Report at the CFTC Website (08:49)
The COT website automatically updates the members section weekly with real-time data at approximately 3:00PM EST every Friday. However, this video demonstrates how you can also locate the COT data for the Euro FX manually at the CFTC website.

9.5. Date and Commercial Contracts Explanation (22:31)
Under the Euro FX report, the first two main columns titled Date and Commercial Contracts are explained. The sub-columns discussed under the Date column are 'WEEKS FR LAS JAN 01' and 'DAY MOS YEAR'. The sub-columns discussed under the Commercial Contracts column are 'NET QTY LNG-SHT', 'NET CHG FR PREV', 'NET COMM INDEX', 'QTY LONG', and "QTY SHORT'.

9.6. Speculator Contracts Explanation (11:55)
Under the Euro FX report, the third main column titled Speculator Contracts is explained. The sub-columns discussed under the Speculator Contracts column are 'NET QTY LNG-SHT', 'NET CHG FR PREV', 'NET SPECUL INDEX', 'QTY LONG', and "QTY SHORT'.

9.7. Small Trader Explanation (17:09)

Under the Euro FX report, the fourth main column titled Small Trader is explained. The sub-columns discussed under the Speculator Contracts column are 'NET QTY LNG-SHT', 'NET CHG FR PREV', 'NET SMALL INDEX', 'QTY LONG', and "QTY SHORT'.

9.8. Open Interest and Future Price Explanation (05:41)

Under the Euro FX report, the remaining sub-columns titled 'OPEN INTEREST', 'OPEN INT CHG FR PREV', and 'FUTURE PRICE' are explained.

9. Commitment of Traders (COT)
COT Part II

Refer to:
CD Disk 8

9.9. Graph COT Index and Net Position Explanation (29:16)
Under the Euro FX report, the Graph of COT Index & Net Position is explained. The data that is plotted on the graph discussed are 'NET CONTRACTS', 'NET INDEX', 'PRICE INDEX', and 'PRICE PERC'.

9.10. Graph COT Index and Net Position Application (18:04)
Understanding the data represented on the Graph COT Index & Net Position when the Commercial Traders are Extremely Short and Extremely Long.

9.11. Graph COT, Spec, Small Index/Price Explanation (17:25)
Under the Euro FX report, the Graph COT, Spec, Small Index/Price is explained. The data that is plotted on the graph discussed are 'comm index', 'spec index', 'small index', and 'price perc'.

9.12. Graph COT, Spec, Small Index/Price Application (13:17)
Understanding the data represented on the Graph COT Spec, Small Index/Price when the Commercial Traders are Extremely Short and Extremely Long.

9.13. How COT Works 1 (12:50)
Peter explains the dynamics behind commercial trading activity using a conceptual diagram. During the accumulation phase, the commercial traders are buying as price continues to fall. Ultimately a pending price trend reversal will occur and price will rise. As price rises, the commercial traders will sell back their positions they bought previously for a profit. This is known as the distribution phase. As price continue higher, the commercial traders continue to sell until price finds a top and a price trend reversal occurs and price falls. At this point the cycle comes full circle and starts all over again.

9.14. How COT Works 2 (07:21)
Peter explains the dynamics behind commercial trading activity in relation to the speculators and small traders using the Australian Dollar report and AUD/USD daily chart. Peter discusses the

relationship of the data on the Graph COT, Spec, Small Index/Price, and on the Graph COT, Spec, Small Index/Price.

9.15. How COT Works 3 (09:02)
Peter reiterates the dynamics behind commercial trading activity in relation to the speculators and small traders using the Australian Dollar report and AUD/USD daily chart. Peter discusses the relationship of the data on the Graph COT, Spec, Small Index/Price, and on the Graph COT, Spec, Small Index/Price. Portions of this video will have repetitive information to the video How COT Works 2 however, please note the additional comments that Peter makes.

9.16. When to Enter (01:14)
Once COT kicks in, you want to be using sound technical analysis when looking for an optimal entry point and exiting the trade at the appropriate time.

9.17. Be Patient with COT (01:31)
When considering a position based on the information COT is presenting, exercise patience along with the application of sound technical analysis in order to obtain an optimal entry point for a trade.

9.18. Independent Research on COT (00:52)
A submission made by a Forexmentor member in regards to independent research on how effective is COT the results are "astounding." The link for the PDF full article is provided in the video.

Refer to:
CD Disk 8

9. Commitment of Traders (COT)
COT Examples

9.19. Australian Dollar Example 1 (02:01)
Peter evaluates the extreme divergence between the commercial traders and the speculators and small traders on the Australian Dollar. The commercial traders are extremely short whereas the speculators and small traders are extremely long the Australian Dollar. When we have this extreme divergence, there is an increased probability that we will see a price trend reversal

sometime in the future. In this case, a potential fall in the price could occur in the future.

9.20. Australian Dollar Example 2 (05:44)
Peter continues his evaluation of the extreme divergence between the commercial traders and the speculators and small traders on the Australian Dollar. The commercial traders are extremely short whereas the speculators and small traders are extremely long the Australian Dollar. When we have this extreme divergence, there is an increased probability that we will see a price trend reversal sometime in the future. In this case, a potential fall in the price could occur in the future. Use sound technical analysis to determine a top and to look for an optimal entry point.

9.21. Australian Dollar Example 3 (02:36)
Peter continues his evaluation of the extreme divergence between the commercial traders and the speculators and small traders on the Australian Dollar. The commercial traders are extremely short whereas the speculators and small traders are extremely long the Australian Dollar. Use sound technical analysis to determine a top and to look for an optimal entry point.

9.22. Australian Dollar Example 4 (05:18)
Peter continues his evaluation of the extreme divergence between the commercial traders and the speculators and small traders on the Australian Dollar. The price trend reversal has come to fruition and the Australian Dollar has fallen in price.

9.23. Australian Dollar Example Brag Time (03:01)
Who could have guessed? It's shameless brag time. COT strikes again!

COT

Personal Notes and Observations

Part II

Putting the Tools to Work

Top Down Trading
(Working Through a Trade)

Now that you have an understanding of how some of the basic technical analysis tools work, you need to know how to start using them. You could use any one of the technical tools by itself. However, doing that would most likely result in many losing trades. Remember, we are looking for a "confluence of events" to make our trading decisions.

The top down trading method is a way of analyzing price starting at a higher time frame and working towards a lower time frame. This method helps you to see the big picture. By seeing the big picture, you will be more likely to find higher probability trades.

As you do this analysis in your own trading, you will find that it is helpful to keep certain support and resistance lines on your weekly, daily and 4-hour charts for quite some time, in some cases months, in other cases years. The technical markings on your 60 minute and 15 minute charts will be very dynamic, most likely changing almost everyday.

Top down trading is the path to trading success, so please try to follow along with us as we set up a trade using some of the technical tools we have learned.

We start with taking a look at the weekly chart. (See diagram **TDT1.0**)

First, we should start by saying that there's no real benefit to look at the indicators on the weekly chart due to the fact we are not looking for long term position trades that may be held for weeks, months or years. What we are going to look for are 'key' or 'major' points of support and resistance and the overall trend. Although, there will be price patterns that appear in this time frame, they will also appear on the daily chart and that is where we will look to see how we should trade those price patterns in a shorter time frame.

In **TDT1.0**, we have inserted a black (thick) support line, which is based on the price levels of points 1 and 2. We have also inserted two red (thin) resistance lines based on points 3 and 4.

Again, these support and resistance points are what we use the weekly time frame to find and note.

TDT1.0 – Looking for Support and Resistance Levels

The next time frame that we will look at is the daily chart. (See diagram **TDT1.1**) We actually look at the daily chart in *two* different ways:

The first way is to look at the daily chart where the candles are compressed very close together. This is where we look to see chart patterns that would indicate a trend reversal. We would want to note that this chart shows the EURUSD to be in an uptrend that was initiated by the inverted head and shoulders. (See diagram **TDT1.1**) Line **#1** is the neckline of the inverted head and shoulders. Lines **#2** and **#3** are showing us a falling wedge that is occurring in an uptrend (not commented on in the course; go to www.chartpatterns.com for more information) which is usually a bullish indicator, meaning that price should continue to go back up.

TDT1.1 – Daily Chart Compressed

The second way we look at the daily chart is to expand it out a bit so that we can see the candles more clearly and to better prepare us for our trade setup for the day. We have identified two major trend lines in **TDT1.2** and would want to pay close attention to our lower time frame charts when price gets close to either one of the trendlines to determine the probability of whether price will bounce off the trendline or break through it. We would also note that the MACD lines are right on the neutral line, not giving us much information. However, we would want to note that the stochastic indicator is in the overbought area. And the 1.2700 area, where the orange (horizontal) line is, has been very strong support and resistance. Price is currently above that level and it could come back down close to it and test it again as support. Again, we must be aware of what is happening on the daily chart in order to make *better* decisions on the lower time frame charts.

TDT1.2 – Daily Chat Expanded

The next time frame chart that we will look at is the 240 minute or the 4 hour chart. (See diagram **TDT1.3**)

Some charting services may not provide a chart with this time frame so you may try substituting the 120 minute or 2-hour chart in its place. We would first want to notice the orange support line, at the 1.2700 level on the chart that we added from the daily chart. Then we would want to draw the upper and lower blue trendlines and note that price is near the lower trendline.

The MACD is just following price like it is supposed to, slightly turning down with price, and the stochastic is heading toward the oversold area. Not too much more than that for us on this chart.

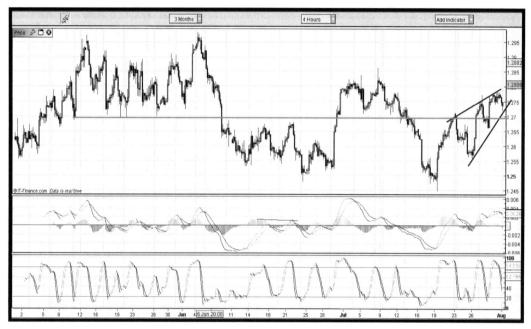

TDT1.3 – 240 Minute or 4 Hour Chart

Now we will check the 1 hour chart. (See diagram **TDT1.4**)

We note the *same* two blue trendlines. Price is right on the lower trendline and looks to be pushing through it a bit. MACD is heading down. What else do you see? Is the stochastic in the oversold area? Has it curled up a bit? With price down at 1.2729 and slowly closing in on that strong support area of 1.2700, price could move quickly through the trendline and then go back up (watch for this, it happens but our stochastic helps us to not sucked in by this).

TDT1.4 – 1 Hour Chart

Now we will take a quick look at the 5-minute chart. We will first add the Central Pivot to get an idea where price is in reference to the other pivot points. We notice that price is below the Central Pivot, which would place us in the 'buy' area of the pivot system. We also note that the MACD is showing us a bit of divergence as noted by the lines on diagram **TDT1.5**. Notice too, that the stochastic is near the oversold area and heading there but not there yet, suggesting that price may pull down a bit.

TDT1.5 – 5 Minute Chart

Now we look at the 15-minute chart with the other pivots added to it. We have labeled the Central Pivot and the closest M-level pivots. Notice that we have some railroad track candle patterns. MACD is just doing its job of following price with no divergence. Stochastic is coming out of the oversold area and we are in the buy area of the pivots. (See diagram **TDT1.6**)

TDT1.6 – 15 Minute Chart

So what should we be thinking?
We know we are near the strong support of 1.2700.
We are right on a major lower trendline.
We have a railroad tracks candle pattern, at the London open.
We have several time frames where the stochastic is near or at the bottom.
We are in the buy area of the pivots, near M1 on a M1/M3 day.

We should consider going *long* the EUR/USD pair, meaning we are expecting the chart to turn back up.

So maybe we plan to buy the EUR/USD around 1.2720, near M1. Place a stop at 1.2695, on the other side of the strong support. And since we are new at this, set a price target of 20-25 pips at 1.2745. What would happen if that was our trade? (See diagram **TDT1.7**)

Within a couple of hours our trade was closed for a profit. Price actually ran up to 1.2800. But because we are new traders, we fight off greedy and focus on making good trading decisions. This will eventually lead to steady growth of our trading account.

TDT1.7 – Trade was Closed for a Profit

What does this mean to us? A pip is the smallest *increment* a currency is traded in. Every currency has its own 'pip' value. For the EUR/USD, if you are trading one *standard lot,* each pip is equal to $10. If you are trading a *mini lot*, each pip is equal to $1. So if the EUR/USD goes from 1.2720 to 1.2745 it has moved 25 pips upwards. If you 'buy' the EUR/USD, which means you are 'long' the EUR, and it goes up, you make 25 pips of profit. If you are trading one standard EUR/USD lot, that equals $250 profit. If you are trading one mini EUR/USD lot, that equals $25 profit. If you are trading multiple lots—you can do the math.

Can you see how doing the top down analysis can help you get a good picture of what is going on in the market? And how profitable this type of trading can be?

Refer to:
CD Disk 9

10. Top Down Trading
<u>Top Down Trading</u>

10.1. Top Down Trading 1 (05:29)
Peter explains the concept of top-down trading using a pictorial diagram representing the daily, hourly, 15 minute & 5 minute chart.

10.2. Top Down Trading 2 (01:16)
Peter explains the concept of top-down trading using a more detailed pictorial diagram representing the daily, hourly, 15 minute & 5 minute chart.

10.3. Top Down Trading Example 1 (21:55)
Peter explains the concept of top-down trading using the EUR/USD daily, hourly & 15 minute chart. Peter runs through this example in great detail. This is a good lesson in understanding the thought process of Peter and how he applies his system when analyzing the EUR/USD. The application of the concept remains the same in which you start looking at higher timeframes and continue down to lower timeframes enabling you to draw a conclusion of what the current trend of the currency pair is. For more information on the various price projection methods, please visit the Video Tutorial Library in the Forexmentor member's area.

10.4. Top Down Trading Example 2 (10:01)
Peter explains the concept of top-down trading using the EUR/USD daily, hourly & 15 minute chart. Peter runs through this example in great detail. This is a good lesson in understanding the thought process of Peter and how he applies his system when analyzing the EUR/USD. Additionally, the concept of selling the rallies in a downtrend will be included in this example.

10.5. Top Down Trading and Timeframes (00:53)
When position trading, you should focus more on the higher level charts such as the monthly, weekly & daily chart, and use the 15 or 5 minute chart to execute trades. When day trading, your focus will be more on the 4 hour, hourly and 15 minute charts.

10.6. Top Down Analysis in Short Term Trading (01:27)
When using the concept of top down trading for short term trades,

your focus will predominately be on the hourly & 15 minute chart.

10.7. Reading the Charts Top Down (02:58)
When looking at a currency pair using top down analysis, you are not going to see the same things on all the timeframes.

10. Top Down Trading
Confluence of Events

10.8. The 21 Pieces of the Confluence Puzzle (01:00)
A list of the most significant factors to taken into consideration when looking for a confluence of events in order to make a trading decision.

10.9. Confluence of Events Reminder (01:44)
Peter reminds us that you just can't focus on one aspect such as a trendline break when making a trading decision but to look for a confluence of events.

10.10. The Perfect Peter Bain Trade 1 (02:43)
An example of a "perfect Peter Bain trade" on the EUR/USD 15 minute chart submitted by a Forexmentor member who made a successful trading decision based on a confluence of events.

10.11. The Perfect Peter Bain Trade 2 (06:41)
Additional comments from Peter regarding an example of a "perfect Peter Bain trade" on the EUR/USD 15 minute chart submitted by a Forexmentor member who made a successful trading decision based on a confluence of events.

10.12. Confluence of Indicators (02:08)
An example of a confluence of events on the EUR/USD hourly chart.

10.13. Understanding Confluence (01:47)
An example of a confluence of events on the EUR/USD using the Daily, 4 hour & 15 minute chart submitted by Vic Noble.

10.14. Using Confluence Examples (05:01)
Examples of confluence of events on the USD/CHF, GBP/USD & EUR/USD 15 minute charts submitted by a Forexmentor member.

10.15. Detecting Confluence Using Side by Side Charts (03:16)
A Forexmentor member describes how they use charts side by side of the EUR/USD & GBP/USD to determine a confluence of events in order to make a trading decision.

Refer to:
CD Disk 10

10. Top Down Trading
Historical Trading Examples

10.16. February 17, 2005 (15:24)
Peter's commentary of price action on the EUR/USD 15 minute chart. Good example of TD trendlines and hammers.

10.17. February 23, 2005 (08:28)
Peter's commentary of price action on the EUR/USD 15 & 5 minute charts. Good example of TD trendlines, M2/M4 and MACD positive divergence.

10.18. February 24, 2005 (08:55)
Peter's commentary of price action on the EUR/USD 15 & 5 minute charts. Good example of TD trendlines, RR tracks, pivot points and MACD negative divergence.

10.19. March 1, 2005 (05:27)
Peter's commentary of price action on the EUR/USD hourly & 15 minute charts. Good example of TD trendlines, RR tracks, hammer, pivot points and MACD negative divergence.

10.20. March 2, 2005 (14:37)
Peter's commentary of price action on the EUR/USD 15 minute chart. Good example of TD trendlines and triangle.

10.21. March 3, 2005 (07:40)
Peter's commentary of price action on the EUR/USD 15 minute chart. Good example of TD trendlines, M1/M3, Double Bottom and MACD positive divergence.

10.22. March 4, 2005 (07:03)
Peter's commentary of price action on the EUR/USD 15 minute chart. Good example of TD trendlines, hammer, Double Bottom,

pivot points and MACD positive divergence.

10.23. March 10, 2005 (05:20)
Peter's commentary of price action on the EUR/USD 15 minute chart. Good example of TD trendlines, pivot points and London Open.

10.24. March 24, 2005 (10:58)
Peter's commentary of price action on the EUR/USD 15 & 5 minute charts. Good example of TD trendlines, hammer RR tracks and M1/M3

10.25. March 25, 2005 (12:20)
Peter's commentary of price action on the GBP/USD 15 & 5 minute charts. Good example of TD trendlines, hammer, M1/M3 and pivot points.

10.26. March 29, 2005 (06:26)
Peter's commentary of price action on the EUR/USD 15 & 5 minute charts. Good example of TD trendlines, double top, London open, pivot points, hammers, spinning top and MACD negative divergence.

10.27. March 31, 2005 (07:08)
Peter's commentary of price action on the EUR/USD 15 & 5 minute charts. Good example of TD trendlines, double top, pivot points, hammer and MACD negative divergence.

10.28. April 7, 2005 (11:30)
Peter's commentary of price action on the GBP/USD 15 & 5 minute charts. Good example of TD trendlines, 1-2-3 Top, pivot points, London open and M2/M4.

10.29. April 28, 2005 (12:31)
Peter's commentary of price action on the EUR/USD Daily, hourly & 15 minute charts. Good example of TD trendlines and triangle.

10.30. May 3, 2005 (10:13)
Peter's commentary of price action on the EUR/USD hourly, 15 & 5 minute charts. Good example of TD trendlines, price projections and MACD positive divergence.

10.31. May 4, 2005 (03:02)
Peter's commentary of price action on the EUR/USD 15 minute chart. Good example of TD trendlines, hammer, and London Open.

10.32. May 5, 2005 (16:03)
Peter's commentary of price action on the EUR/USD 15 & 5 minute charts. Good example of TD trendlines, hammer, RR tracks and pivot points.

10.33. May 6, 2005 (05:13)
Peter's commentary of price action on the EUR/USD 15 & 5 minute charts. Good example of TD trendlines, hammer, pivot points and MACD positive divergence.

10.34. May 10, 2005 (08:16)
Peter's commentary of price action on the EUR/USD hourly, 15 & 5 minute charts. Good example of hammer pivot points and M2/M4

10.35. May 11, 2005 (09:51)
Peter's commentary of price action on the GBP/USD 15 & 5 minute charts. Good example of TD trendlines, RR tracks and pivot points.

10.36. May 12, 2005 (13:18)
Peter's commentary of price action on the EUR/USD Daily, hourly, 15 & 5 minute charts. Good example of MACD neutralization and pivot points.

10.37. May 13, 2005 (10:24)
Peter's commentary of price action on the GBP/USD hourly & 15 minute charts. Good example of TD trendlines and M1/M3.

Top Down Trading

Personal Notes and Observations

Risk Management

It is impossible to overemphasize the importance of proper risk management. There is a reason why brokers offer enormous margins. Sure, the fact that because they can afford to is a simple answer, but it also allows traders to get in way over their heads and lose money fast. Smart traders will never risk anything even close to the 200:1 margins offered by many of the retail brokers. While this is an obvious point, it is only the tip of the iceberg when it comes to proper risk management. Simply put, proper risk management will keep you in this business. It will help you keep your losses within reason, while making the most of your gains.

Let's begin with how much of your capital you should risk. Risk management is based upon percentages of your capital in various ways and it begins with the maximum amount of capital that you will risk at any given time. Professional traders risk *between* 0.5% to 2% per trade. How do you expect to make your living at trading if you risk more than the professionals. Most novice traders begin by risking much more than the pros in an attempt to get bigger returns quickly.

The most typical reason for this is because they are *focusing* on potential returns rather than *prioritizing* the protection of capital. In other words, a novice will come to the market at the beginning of a given month and say, I have $20,000.00 USD in my account and I need to make $5,000.00 USD this month in order to pay my bills. This means that I need to make 25% this month, and in order to do so I'll need to risk a large amount of my capital in order to get there by the end of the month. Can you figure out why so many traders wash out of the market when their real intention is to make all the money they need to live on?

Professional traders use proper risk management that prioritizes the protection of their capital in order to live to fight another day. As mentioned above, they will *rarely* risk more than 0.5 to 2% at any given time. This is probably one of the most important points in this text. If you can't provide for yourself as a full time trader using these kinds of percentages, then keep your day job until you can!

11. Risk Management
Risk Management

Refer to:
CD Disk 11

11.1. Money Management Considerations (02:19)
Please keep in mind the following suggestions from Peter in this video.

Homework - Do It or Get Schooled

We live in a time when there is more information available to more people on the planet then ever before. People are consuming information at a staggering pace. A person needs to recognize there is a difference between *consuming* information and *processing* information. Consuming information can lead to absolutely no benefits; it can go in one ear and out the other.

Processing information, on the other hand, requires thought and meditation, which will lead to positive results. For a trader, the best way to start doing this is by keeping a trading journal.

Those that succeed in trading are those that work at it. There are no shortcuts in this business. So if you are used to getting by on short cuts in your daily life, prepare to make some small changes or the market will cut you short. Make sure you do your top down analysis prior to a trade and review a trade thoroughly afterwards. Take good notes and keep good logs. Do you think it is the 90% who wash out of trading that do their homework or the 10% who succeed?

Refer to:
CD Disk 11

12. Homework – Do it of Get Schooled
<u>Homework</u>

12.1. Keep a Log (01:18)
If it isn't written, it doesn't exist. Record everything you do in a journal.

12.2. Write Things Down (00:30)
When you stop writing things down, you are going to fail! You can't wing it when trading.

12.3. The Importance of Taking Notes (04:10)
Are you writing things down? You must be disciplined. You need to write things down.

12.4. Setting Up a Trading Log (01:20)
An example of a Forexmentor member's detailed trading log.

12.5. Keeping a Trading Journal (01:33)
Another example of a trading journal checklist.

Here are a couple of questions to ask yourself:

Would you let an experienced doctor who had just read a book on heart surgery operate on you? Even though he has experience as a doctor, does that experience qualify him to do heart surgery?

Believe it or not, with no experience, people give them themselves permission to do things they would never let anyone else do. Spend some time thinking about those questions and honestly evaluating your trading skills *before* you start to trade your hard-earned money in the markets.

Almost every occupation demands that you complete some type of continuing education requirement over a certain period of time; trading should be no different. You must develop an education plan. If you are not sure how to develop one or what to include in one, ask a trader that has some experience that can evaluate your current status and give you some suggestions based on your personal life style and goals.

12. Homework – Do it of Get Schooled
Homework

Refer to:
CD Disk 11

12.6. Printing AM Review Slides (02:50)
Instructions on how to invert the color scheme of the AM Review Slides in order to save ink on your printer when printing out the AM Review Slides for private study.

12.7. Crosschecking Your Work (01:44)
It is always important to cross-check your work. However if you do make a mistake, and you do take a loss, consider it a part of you ongoing education, and learn from your mistakes.

Patience

Many of the skills that we've discussed to this point involve patience. It is something that all good traders are constantly battling. There are many unique aspects to the job of a professional trader, but one of them is that payday is *not* the 2nd and last Friday of each month. In fact, it is hard to know when we will be paid for all of our hard work. This can cause a big psychological barrier and is the reason that many traders lose a lot of money. Let's explain further.

A trader can work hard day after day, but never execute a trade. Meanwhile our bills continue to stack up. We need to buy groceries, fill the car with gas, etc. Somewhere in the back of our mind, we start thinking that we will need to be paid eventually. At that point, we find ourselves entering what may be a decent looking trade, but it's not an ideal setup according to our system. We enter a trade and quickly find ourselves with a loss. What happened? In short, the market out waited us and the market beat us. It's very difficult but good traders do not get out-waited by the market, they exercise patience and let their setups develop, often for days and sometimes for weeks.

Patience also comes into play once you finally do see a setup and enter a trade. Sometimes the market will seem to drift along endlessly, particularly for a more novice trader who might not have their entry points honed just yet. But even the seasoned trader is subjected to a slow market from time to time. Don't expect the market to move your trade positive right after you click the mouse and execute your position. This is *not* necessarily a sign that the market is going to move against you. Be PATIENT and follow your plan. Let the indicators help you decide if the market still is set up to move with you. Along the same lines, don't let the market wait you out even if you are in a positive trade. Stick with your targets and let your system tell you if it's time to get out.

Patience is important in all aspects of trading. It's necessary to be patient while you are learning the skills in this book. It also takes patience to stay in a trade while the market moves slowly at times. Don't let the market out wait you!

Refer to:
CD Disk 11

13. Patience
<u>Patience</u>

13.1. Patience to Wait for Opportunities (01:35)
Nine common denominators shared by the successful traders interviewed by Jack Schwager in his book Market Wizards.

13.2. It All Takes Time (01:12)
Do you have a trading plan? It takes time to understand the market. You can't just jump into currency trading and expect results immediately.

13.3. Patience Folks (02:29)
Trading currencies is NOT like kangaroos jumping up and down on speed! Price doesn't just drop like a stone. It saw-tooth's it way down. Look for rallies to sell in the downtrend.

13.4. Impatience Can Kill You (00:26)
ICKY, or in the case of a trading account, can cause you to go broke.

13.5. Patience (03:17)
The learning curve can take anywhere from six months to three years. Trading currencies is no different then your current career. There is a steep learning curve. It takes time.

Part III

Things You Need to Know About the Forex

What is Forex and What is a Pip?

What is Foreign Exchange (Forex)?

Simply put, foreign exchange is the changing of one currency for another for a period of time. Have you ever gone on vacation to another nation and exchanged your home nation's money for that of the country that you are visiting? That exchange did occur on the foreign exchange market.

The Forex market is unique in 3 very important ways.

1) Accessibility: No special license needed, a "seat" on any exchange or any "formal" education in order to participate in trading. This can be very dangerous, so please take your time and monitor your education very carefully!

2) The Forex market is completely decentralized. There is no bricks and mortar building in which the market is located. Anyone with a computer and an internet connection, or a phone for that matter can open an account with a broker (assuming that they meet minimal application requirements) and place a trade in the Forex market.

3) The Forex market is vastly larger than any other financial market in the world. In fact, it is larger than all of the other financial markets in the world combined with an average of over 1.7 trillion US Dollars exchanging hands every day of the week!

So why do we care about these three attributes? Because just like a boxer enters the ring with an understanding of who their opponent is, or a chess player is constantly trying to read their competitor for clues as to their strategy, it is important to understand who you are dealing with when you choose to participate in this market.

There are no pit traders to gun your stops, and no insiders to step on your toes. But it is a huge arena with huge players! It operates through a global network of national banks, commercial banks, global corporations and individuals trading one currency for another. The lack of a physical exchange enables the Forex market to operate around the clock, spanning the world from one major financial center to the next.

The Forex market is driven by real need and real economic forces between countries and the economic sectors of the world. National banks act to protect their national currency, create favourable exchange rates for importers and exporters, and hedge their debts. International portfolio managers, multinational corporations, long-term holders and hedge funds all use the Forex market to pay for goods and services, transact in financial assets, or to reduce the risk of currency movements by hedging their exposure in other markets.

These are 'the Big Dogs' – they own most of the world's money, and they are doing business, not playing a game.

The role of the small speculator – that's you – is insignificant in the grand scheme of the market. The thousands of dollars you can make, by acting nimbly in the direction the market is going, will never be missed by the larger players.

The Currency Pairs

In the Forex market, currencies are quoted in pairs for the purpose of creating an environment for trading. Approximately 85% of the total volume of this market takes place in the four major currency pairs. They are the:

EUR/USD or "the Euro"
USD/JPY or "the Yen"
GBP/USD or "the Pound"
USD/CHF or "the Swiss Franc"

The first currency in the pair is the "dominant" currency, and the second is the "subordinate" or quoted currency. The quoted currency is the one that is given by the dealer. For example, in the case of the EUR/USD at the time of this writing, the quote is;

EUR / USD = 1.2730 / 1.2733

In the above example, 1.2730 is the *sell price* and the 1.2733 is the *buy price*.

This is the current value of the US Dollar versus the Euro. A simpler way to look at it is that it currently costs $1.2730 to buy a single Euro. Now you should be asking yourself, why are there two different prices? The reason is that the broker offers both a *sell price* and a *buy price*. The difference between the two prices is called the *spread* and this is where the broker makes their money. It is important to note that not all spreads are the same.

Refer to:
CD Disk 12

14. What is Forex and What is a Pip
The Currency Pairs

14.1. The Mechanics of the Trading Pairs (00:33)
Peter reiterates how the relationship between the currency pairs works using 3 examples and Peter also shows you how to determine profit & loss.

14.2. Trading Pairs Terminology (00:54)
You have to get use to the terminology in reference to currency pairs in newspapers, news feeds, etc...

14.3. Pip Spreads (03:30)
Peter explains how the pip spread works.

14.4. The Four Major Pairs (01:25)
85% of all trading volume in the Forex is represented by the four major pairs. Peter recommends you to pick one, and specialize in it.

14.5. Most Active Pairs (00:52)
Here we have a pie chart diagram courtesy Bank for International Settlements depicting the most active currency pairs for the Tokyo and London session. The Tokyo session is mostly dominated by the USD/JPY pair and for the London session we have the EUR/USD & GBP/USD occupying the bulk of the trading activity. This is good information to know when you are determining which currency pair(s) you choose to trade.

14.6. Which Pair Should I Specialize In (00:37)
A Forexmentor member residing in London, UK, asks which currency pair should they specialize in and Peter offers up the solution to take into consideration depending on which session they choose to trade, pick the currency pair that predominately occupies the most volume for that session.

Pips

A *pip* is simply one numeric move in the last digit in the quote. In the above example, a change from 1.2730 to 1.2731 would be a change of one pip. The broker's "commission" is paid on the spread of 3 pips between the sell price and buy price. Pips are essentially the Forex version of a tick in commodity futures.

Refer to:
CD Disk 12

14. What is Forex and What is a Pip
<u>Pips</u>

14.7. What is a Pip (00:34)
Using the EUR/USD 15 Minute chart, Peter explains what a pip is.

14.8. Pip Values (00:37)
Peter shows the pip values for the four major currency pairs.

14.9. Pip Values Updated (01:09)
Peter explains the pip values for the currency pairs and reiterates what a pip is.

What Moves the Forex Market

The movement of capital between countries is the main factor determining the current state of the market. Within that movement, factors being considered are balances of mutual payments, national economic conditions, political policy, forecasts based on technical analysis, as well as psychological factors. Currency prices are affected by a variety of economic and political conditions, but probably the most important are interest rates, inflation and political stability.

All of the factors mentioned above may cause sudden and often dramatic shifts in the market if some unexpected or considerable changes occur in them. As you have seen on any intraday chart the market is not static for very long and is usually fluctuating from moment to moment. These fluctuations show the markets sentiment towards the value of a currency.

So does this mean you have to be fanatic in watching for news and or Government reports? No, it is not necessary, but it is a good idea to know when major announcements are scheduled. Trading with technical indicators will give you your signal and will reflect the content of the news. Usually at the time of any major announcement the market will react with volatility, as traders speculate the effect it will have on any given currency. I advise exercising some patience as usually the aftermath is very often tradable.

15. What Moves the Forex Market
<u>News</u>

Refer to:
CD Disk 12

15.1. Risky Trading the News (01:11)
Two examples of extremely volatile price action at news time in which it would have been more prudent to wait and trade the ensuing momentum after the news.

15.2. The Effect of News (01:56)
An example of the EUR/USD bottoming out after the news release of the retail sales figures. Peter shows you additional clues on why you should have considered going long in the ensuing aftermath of this news event.

Schedules of government reports are available at www.dailyfx.com.

15. What Moves the Forex Market
News

Refer to:
CD Disk 12

15.3. News Source Links (00:38)
You have the choice of using the link for www.dailyfx.com or the link for Market News International.

These are a few of the things which directly influence Forex prices.

Interest Rates

Interest rates are two fold; they determine the "yield" of a currency, while on the other hand they can be viewed as a barometer of the position of a country's economy. Governments use interest rates to try and control inflation, attract foreign investment or stimulate domestic economic growth.

For example, the US has been raising interest rates. This makes investors with interest bearing assets more likely to shift their assets to the US, because they will receive a higher yield. On the other hand, the higher US dollar will hurt exporters because their costs will increase and in turn may slow sales, thereby slowing the US economy. When the economy slows too much, the government will cut interest rates to try and stimulate domestic growth.

Trade

The Forex market exists first and foremost to facilitate trade. The more a country's goods are in demand, therefore requiring buyers to convert their currencies into the exporter's currency, the stronger it will be. It is a simple supply and demand equation. More demand means higher values.

Because of this influence, traders keep an eye on trade data. These figures, of course, are historical by the time you see them. The trade has already happened and the push or pull on a currency's value has already taken place. What traders want to know, however, is what was the change from the previous quarter. Is the money flowing into or out of a country?

Intervention

There are two ways states can control currency. The first one is just control. A country/union can fix its currency value to another currency, thereby not letting it float in the open market. Another method is to prevent citizens from doing anything that can have a negative influence on the exchange rate (for example, transferring money abroad). The second is the so called intervention. Sometimes governments actually participate in the Forex market to influence the value of their currencies, either by flooding the market with their domestic currency in an attempt to lower the price, or, conversely, buying in order to raise the price. This is known as Central Bank intervention. Any of these factors, as well as large market orders, can cause high volatility in currency prices. However, the size and volume of the Forex market makes it impossible for any one entity to "drive" the market for any length of time.

Inflation

The CPI or Consumer Price Index report is the government data that tracks retail prices. Inflation occurs when there is a fall of the market value or purchasing power of money within an economy. This is equivalent to a sustained increase in the general level of prices and is akin to a "cost of living" measurement. When inflation is rising, it reduces the buying power of a currency, especially with regard to other currencies. The US CPI is reported quarterly.

Employment

The government supplies data monthly on the employment rates. Investors use this to determine the economic health of a country/union. A high unemployment rate means slower growth and a weaker economy; vice versa, low unemployment means steady growth and a strong economy. So what is a good number? Investors are not concerned with the actual number itself, but more so with any change from the previous month's data. This change indicates a growing or weakening of a given economy. Watch out for this one folks, it usually creates large price swings in a very small time frame.

15. What Moves the Forex Market
<u>News</u>

Refer to:
CD Disk 12

15.4. Non-Farm Payroll News (01:02)

The non-farm payroll is hands down the most significant market mover, causing an average 124 pip range of trading in the first 20 minutes following the release. Though it maybe very tempting to trade the NFP because of the possibility of making a lot of money in a very short time, price action at these times can be very volatile. It is better to sit on your hands and wait patiently and look for an opportunity to trade the aftermath of this event.

Conclusion

You don't have to be a news junkie, or try to be the first person to hear or read about it. The thing which makes the Forex market so complex is the fact that when one is trying to perform the kind of fundamental analysis we have discussed here, it is a multisided equation. Looking at one country is not enough because a currency is valued and traded against an array of others, all of which have their own sets of considerations. This is why I stress keeping abreast of the news, but trading Technical analysis. You will usually "see" the news in your indicators. The exception to that is "sudden breaking news", terrorist attacks, war, tragedies from Mother Nature to name a few. These will all affect market sentiment and will not give you a warning. This is why you NEVER trade without using a stop loss. These types of situations are not predictable and we need to protect ourselves from the unexpected.

Refer to:
CD Disk 12

15. What Moves the Forex Market
<u>News</u>

15.5. Start of the Iraq War (01:40)
Bombs away! U.S. attacks Iraq at 19:01 on March 19, 2003. A sudden large price spike occurred on the EUR/USD and there is no way you would have known or been prepared for this event. That is why you should always trade with stops.

15.6. Daily Diary of Upcoming Events (00:35)
This website not only gives a daily diary of upcoming events, but also has a history of past events. This is great for back-testing strategies based around news time.

15.7. News Calendar Link (00:29)
Here is another News Calendar you can use. One unique feature is that you can change the time zone to your own time zone and it will automatically convert all the times for you.

15.8. Bloomberg as a News Resource (00:14)
Another powerful news provider.

15.9. Fundamental News Analysis (01:17)
A brief analysis by Peter on fundamental information that was affecting the Euro & Canadian Dollar.

15.10. News Trumping the Technicals (00:41)
Two scenarios submitted by a Forexmentor member showcasing when the fundamentals trump even the most well thought out technical entries.

Your Trading Plan

It is essential that a trader develop a trading plan. Again, we refer to the statistic that 90% of traders wash out of trading. How many of that 90% do you think had a trading plan? When you ask ALL traders if they have a trading plan, less than 10% say that they do. Is there any possibility that there is some connection between the almost 10% who have a trading plan and the almost 10% that succeed in trading?

What a trading plan is not, "I plan to make 50 pips per week"; that is not a plan at all, it is a goal.

A trading plan is a business plan on how you are going to run your trading business. We have listed a sample trading plan with some items you may wish to include. It is by no means exhaustive and do not be afraid to revise it as you develop as a trader.

A Sample Trading Plan

Why Am I Trading?

I am trading because of my passion for the…

What Markets Will I Trade?

I will trade the FX London market with mini lots because…

Why This Market?

I will trade this market because…

What Plays Am I Going To Use

I am going to trade my XXXX trading play during the Asian session, my research and demo testing shows this play to work 76% of the time…

What Is My Trading Psychology

What I am doing to keep my trading psychology is…

Goals:

My personal goals are…

My trading goals are…

My educational goals are…

Profit Rules:

The way I take profit is…

Drawdown Rules:

When my account experiences xxx draw down in xxxx amount of time, I will xxxxxxx with my trading.

Office Setup:

I have a designated work space that will only be used for trading…
I have xxxxx in place for xxxxx technical issues.

What Data Will I Track?

I will track my win to loss ratio and…

I have put together the following spreadsheets for tracking…

Take the time to find some traders who have put together a trading plan. Take the time to put one together; it will serve you well and keep you on target.

16. Your Trading Plan
<u>Trading Plan</u>

Refer to:
CD Disk 12

16.1. Develop Your Own Trading Style (01:01)
Pick a trading plan/style that works for you and tune everybody else out. After all, it's your money.

Choosing a Forex Broker

Choosing a broker is an *important* step in your trading career. You are looking for a broker that you intend to do a lot of business with so it is in your best interest to view them as your business partner.

A good broker, like a good business partner, will want you to succeed in your trading. To help you achieve that success, most brokers offer free demo trading accounts so that you can test drive their trading platform and get familiar with it before using it to trade real money. They also offer tighter spreads and prompt execution of you trades without slippage (a price different than the one you placed your order at). Not all brokers operate their businesses the same so it is up to you to do you due diligence in selecting your business partner.

There are several pieces of information you may want to obtain about your business partner before you start working with them:

- How long have they been in the Forex business?
- What bank are the funds on hand retained at?
- Are the funds pooled with the company's funds or other client's funds or individually segregated?
- Are the funds deposited insured or bonded? If so, for how much?
- Are your accounts audited?
- Will you be a counter party to my trades or are you a direct access broker?
- Do you have trailing stops?
- Do you have a telephone dealing desk?
- What are your margin requirements?
- What time do you use as you end of business day? Is that the same time that interest be charged if there is an interest differential on my open position? Do you pay me the interest on the open position if the interest differential is in my favor?

It is important that you conduct a thorough interview of you potential broker. It might be good to also get some recommendations from experienced traders. When you pick a business partner you want to pick the best one that you can. What happens if after some time you are not happy with the broker you have selected, you can always interview for a new business partner; you are in complete control.

One last item to evaluate in choosing your broker is the test drive of the trading platform they offer. You must be able to operate it comfortably and easily. Take the time to open a demo account with a couple of brokers that you like and see which platform is best for you. Some things to look for:

Do they have free charts with their trading platform?
Can their charts be used on multiple monitors?
Do they have trailing stops?
Do they have live news feeds?

Remember it is always easier to be in business with a good partner; make your choice wisely.

Refer to:
CD Disk 12

17. Choosing a Forex Broker
Forex Broker

17.1. Picking a Forex Broker (00:56)
When choosing a market maker broker, the charts come last! Do your due diligence top-down.

17.2. Broker, Charting and Execution Software Example (02:22)
An example of a Forexmentor member's choice of a broker, charting platform, and third-party order execution software.

How to Place a Trade

There are only two things we do in the market; we buy and sell. Sometimes we open a position by making a buy and we close it by making a sell. Other times will open a position by making a sell and we close it by making a buy. Besides our analysis, that is about all we do.

Many people get confused about the paring of the currencies and how they appear on the chart. For now we will look at this from a very simplistic point of view.

If we see any currency chart and the technical analysis we do suggests that the chart is going to go up, we click 'buy' to enter our trade for that pair. If we see any currency chart and the technical analysis we do suggests that the chart is going to go down, we click 'sell' to enter a trade for that pair.

Let's say that we were looking at diagram **HPT1.0** and our analysis was for the chart to go down, what would you do to enter a profitable trade? SELL, regardless of what the currency pair is. Let's take a look, what if the chart was the currency pair of:

EURUSD? You would SELL and be selling the EUR.
EURJPY? You would SELL and be selling the EUR.
USDJPY? You would SELL and be selling the USD.
GBPUSD? You would SELL and be selling the GBP.
GBPEUR? You would SELL and be selling the GBP
USDCAD? You would SELL and be selling the USD.

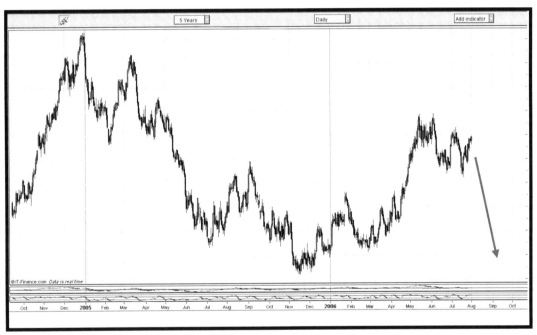

HPT1.0 – Sell the Currency Pair

Let's say that we were looking at diagram **HPT1.1** and our analysis was for the chart to go up, what would you do to enter a profitable trade? BUY, regardless of what the currency pair is. Let's take a look, what if the chart was the currency pair of:

EURUSD? You would BUY and be buying the EUR.
EURJPY? You would BUY and be buying the EUR.
USDJPY? You would BUY and be buying the USD.
GBPUSD? You would BUY and be buying the GBP.
EURGBP? You would BUY and be buying the EUR.
USDCAD? You would BUY and be buying the USD.

HPT1.1 – Buy the Currency Pair

Market Order

When you want to open a trade, you have two choices; one of them is a market order. A market order will give you the best price currently your broker is dealing. When you open a trade using a market order, you are telling your broker, 'get me in the trade now any way you can'. The caution with this type of order is that the broker can give you a *worse* price than you may anticipate; not always, but it can happen.

Limit Entry Order

The other choice you have when opening an order it to use a limit order. You use this when price has not come to the place where you want to enter a trade. You tell the broker, 'when the price gets to this specific price I am telling you, open my trade'. You are essentially placing your trade order in advance. When you use this type of order to get into a trade, you get the exact order you requested.

18. How to Place a Trade
Limit Entry Order

Refer to:
CD Disk 12

18.1. Buy Limit Entry Order (04:16)
An example of a scenario on the GBP/USD 15 Minute Chart in which one would consider using a Buy Limit Entry Order to enter a position.

18.2. Sell Limit Entry Order (03:53)
An example of a scenario on the GBP/USD 15 Minute Chart in which one would consider using a Sell Limit Entry Order to enter a position.

Limit Order

This is an order you place at a price level you expect to take profit if price moves in the directions you anticipate it to. This order is only executed to close a trade that you have opened, at a price specified by you.

18. How to Place a Trade
Limit Order

Refer to:
CD Disk 12

18.3. Buy Limit Order (03:39)
An example of a scenario on the GBP/USD 15 Minute Chart in which one would consider using a Buy Limit Order to take profit.

18.4. Sell Limit Order (02:46)
An example of a scenario on the GBP/USD 15 Minute Chart in which one would consider using a Sell Limit Order to take profit.

Stop Order

This is an order you place at a price level you wish to have you trade closed for a loss if price moves against your open trade. A stop order is like an insurance policy to protect you in the event you either make a bad trading decision or something causes price to move against your trade.

Please take the time to choose a broker based on your personal preferences and their reputation. And please, take the time necessary to learn your brokers trading platform.

Refer to:
CD Disk 12

18. How to Place a Trade
<u>Stop Order</u>

18.5. The Importance of Using Stops (01:05)
Using stop loss orders allow you to be less emotionally involved in your trades. The real reason people don't use stops is that they can't, or won't, admit they were wrong about the trade.

18.6. The Cardinal Rule on Stops (01:33)
Put your stop on and 'stop' fooling around with it. Make a trading decision and stick with it.

18.7. Moving the Stop Order (00:46)
Don't move your stop unless you are trailing it. Once you make a trading decision, put your stop on and leave it there.

18.8. Be Patient and Leave Your Stop Alone (01:09)
Don't second guess your trading decision once you have made it. Leave your stop alone. Price will often retrace to test your patience level.

18.9. Average Stop Order for the Majors (00:19)
Please note that this suggestion is just a general guideline.

18.10. Definition of Trailing Stop (00:57)
Peter explains what a trailing stop is and illustrates how one might use it.

18.11. How to Place Trailing Stops (01:40)

Two trading examples submitted by Forexmentor members illustrating their use of trailing stops.

How to Set Up Your Charts

As we have and will mention one of the wonderful things about learning to trade the Forex is that there are so many FREE resources to use to learn. We will show you how to setup some free basic charts to help you with your trading.

1. Type the following link - http://www.cbfx.com/charts/chartsdemo.htm into your web browser to get to the page you see in diagram **CHART1.0**.

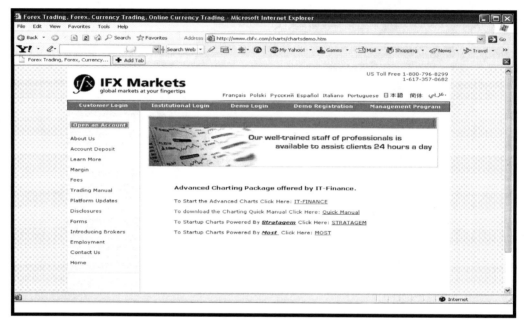

CHART1.0

2. If you do not see the diagram **CHART1.1** come up right away, you many need to download a Sun JAVA applet for Windows. Just type that into Google and you will find the download. It may then ask you if you want to run the JAVA applet before diagram **CHART1.1** comes up, you should click yes. Once you get to diagram **CHART1.1**, you just need to highlight the currency pair you wish to open a chart for and then click 'open a new chart'. A chart should open for you. You can always come back to this page and open as many new charts as you wish. Remember to click the 'save & exit' button before closing your charts if you want to save all of your note and technical markings that you have made on the charts.

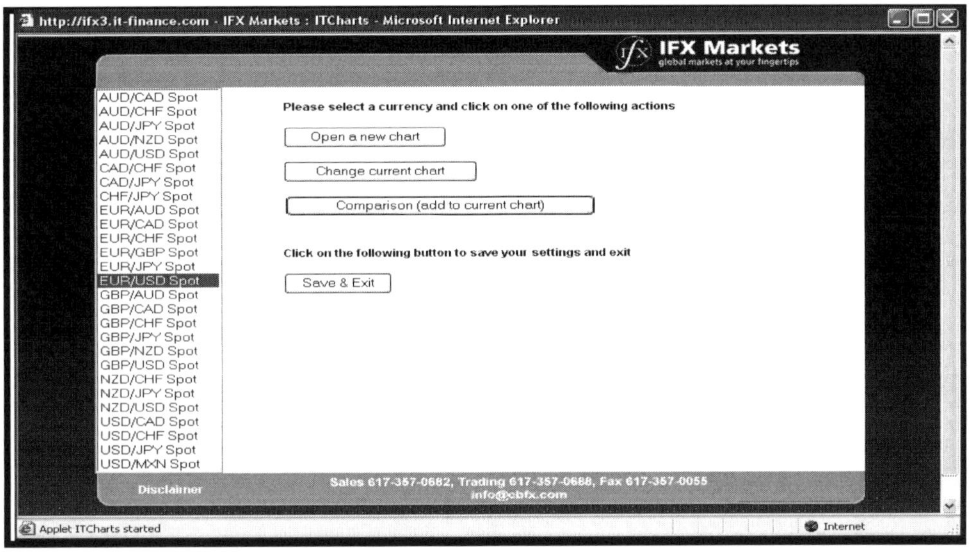

CHART1.1

3. A chart should open like the one you see in diagram **CHART1.2**.

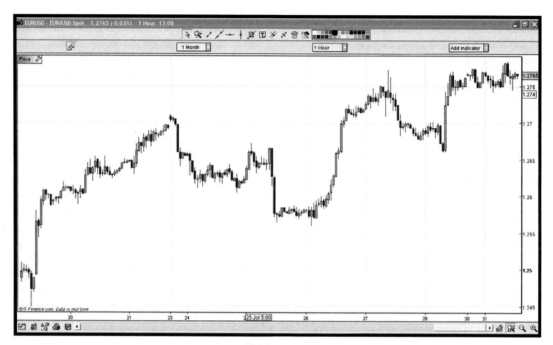

CHART1.2

4. By clicking on the drop down menu with the time in it you can get a selection of different time frames to choose from. (See diagram **CHART1.3**)

CHART1.3

5. By clicking the drop down menu with the other time frame mentioned in it, it will give you a chart looking back over the period of time that you choose. (See diagram **CHART1.4**)

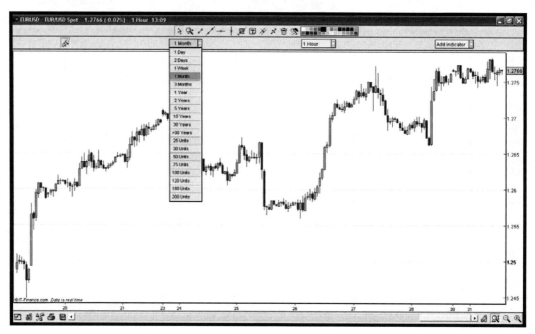

CHART1.4

6. Clicking the "add indicator" drop down menu, in diagram **CHART1.5**, will show you the different indicators you can add to your chart. Just click on the MACD button and the MACD will appear on your chart as you will see in diagram **CHART1.6**.

CHART1.5

7. When the MACD indicator appears on you screen a configuration box will also appear, as seen in diagram **CHART1.6**. We use the normal settings seen here so you can just click "close".

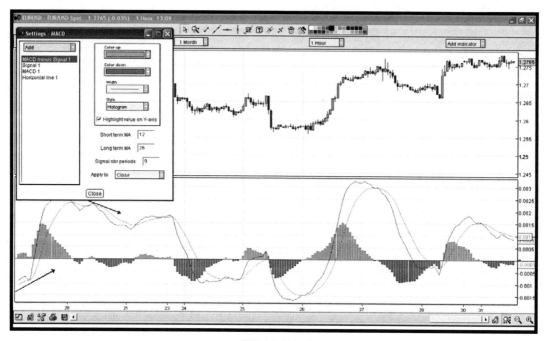

CHART1.6

8. To add another indicator to your chart, go back to the "add indicator drop down menu and click on "stochastic". (See diagram **CHART1.7**)

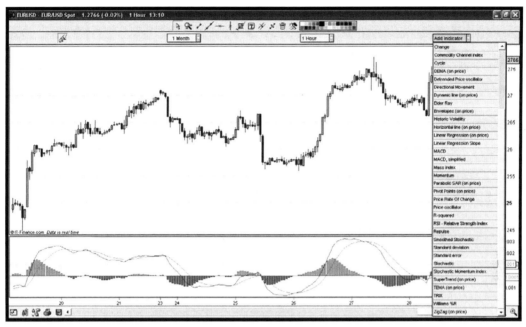

CHART1.7

9. When the stochastic indicator appears, as in diagram **CHART1.8**, you will also see a configuration for the stochastic indicator appear. You should change the settings from 14, 3, 5 to 8, 3, 3 or 5, 3, 3.

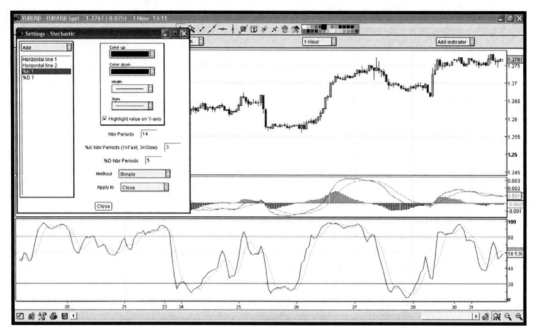

CHART1.8

10. Sometimes you may wish to have a different type of cursor appear on your charts. Click on the little check mark box in the bottom left corner of your chart to bring up the following cursor choice window as seen in diagram **CHART1.9**. Place a check mark next to the type of cursor you would like to have.

You may find it useful to turn on the cross feature by placing a check next to it.

CHART1.9

11. If you click on "open a new chart", you can see in diagram **CHART1.10** how you can have several charts open at once and size them to fit on your computer screen.

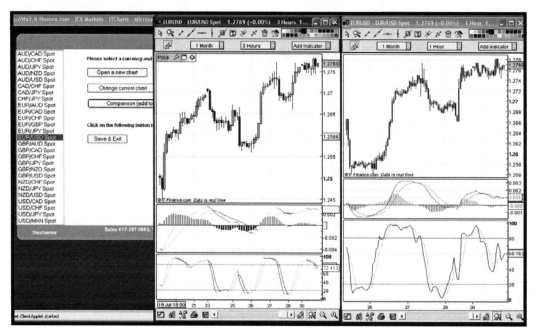

CHART1.10

These few basic tips should help you get some charts up and running so that you can start looking at your currency pairs. You should also note that the broker you sign up with for a demo account may also offer free charting. You will need to download and read their instructions to get your charts running.

Refer to:
CD Disk 12

19. How to Set up Your Charts
Charts Setup

19.1. IT Finance Charts Reference Guide Link (00:24)
The IT Finance charts compact quick manual in PDF Format.

19.2. Drawing Arrows on IT Finance Charts (00:14)
Arrows are a handy tool when making notes on your charts.

19.3. IT Finance Charts Custom Settings (00:36)
Superimposing 2 Stochastics settings one on top of the other, changing MACD lines colors and saving charts.

19.4. Using Templates on IT Finance Charts (01:07)
A 'template' on IT Finance is actually a customizable group of charts, where you can designate 6 to 12 charts as a single template, each of which can have different indicators, settings, periods, etc. Excellent tool for Top-Down analysis for a currency pair.

19.5. How to Simulate Real-Time Using IT Finance Charts (00:24)
Use your IT Finance charts to simulate real-time demo trading. By the end of this exercise, you will get lots and lots of 'in the trenches' practice.

How to Treat Demo Trading

The Forex market is great to learn to trade because so many brokers will give you *free* demo accounts that look and feel like the real platform they offer for trading the real markets with real money. The data feed provided to these demo accounts they offer are based on real market prices. So it is just like trading the real market.

Many traders sign up for these demo accounts and trade large amounts of lots, nothing like they would be prepared to do with their real money, totally depleting a $50,000 account in a few days or weeks. This in no way prepares you to become successful enough to make your living at trading or making any consistent money. If you are learning to fly an airplane with the aid of a flight simulator, what do you gain by recklessly crashing the plane over and over again? Likewise, what do you gain by destroying one demo account after another, over and over again? Your goal should be to get better and better with each demo account.

It is recommended that you always have two demo accounts open at all times. One demo account will be strictly for testing, learning and pulling the trigger when you feel that you 'just have to'. The second demo account should be treated like it is real money. You should only place high probability trades in this account based on your current experience and skill level. Trading your demo accounts in this manner will allow you to see your true progress clearly and properly as you prepare for the time when you will move to trading real money. It is also recommended that you trade a demo account with the same risk per trade and a dollar value that is similar to the amount of money you will have when you open your trading account with real money. Doing this will better prepare you manage the emotions that come when you start trading with real money.

20. How to Treat Demo Trading
Demo Trading

Refer to:
CD Disk 12

20.1. Trade in Your Sandbox Until You See a Trade (02:15)
Keep a demo account for pulling the trigger when you feel that you 'just have to' even after you have successfully transitioned from a demo account to trading real money

What You Should Consider Before Trading REAL Money

You would be amazed at the number of people who start to trade real money and throw everything they have learned out the window and operate in a way that is not in their own best interests. Please take heed of the following thoughts.

There are some considerations you should seriously keep in mind before you start to trade your hard-earned money.

Have you been able to consistently trade successfully in your demo account? If not, you should continue to demo trade until you are consistently making money in your demo account. You would be amazed at the number of people that feel you cannot know what it feels like to really trade unless you trade real money. There is a measure of truth to that, however, would you go out and buy and airplane and just start to fly it? No, you need to practice and the government recognizes this and will not let you fly solo unless you meet certain criteria. Yet, they will let you trade with little to no experience. What would happen if you tried that with and airplane? Do you expect different results from trading real money with little to no experience or guidance? Would you let someone perform surgery on you who had only read a book on how to do open heart surgery? Would you let someone else trade your money who had only read a book on how to trade the markets? Why would you allow yourself to do this with your hard-earned money when you would not let someone else do the same thing? Again, these are some questions you should seriously consider before trading real money to make sure that you are ready to take that step.

Another item to consider is the type of lots you will trade. By trading mini lots, this will provide you with a tremendous amount of agility in trading the Forex market. If your broker does not allow you to trade mini lots, find a new broker.

Taking Care of the Trader

Taking Care of the Trader

As you embark on your Forex trading career, it is quite likely that you also have a day job and an employer that you report to on a regular basis. This employer provides you with a paycheck for your efforts and this paycheck is what you rely on to pay your bills.

With your employer, if you show up to work a little late, or without getting enough rest, you're probably still going to receive that paycheck at the end of the week.

This is NOT the case trading the Forex. If you do not show up to trade in good form, not only will you be unable to generate profits, you could potentially lose money by the end of the week! Your profits will be based on many things; not just what you know about the markets, and we will talk about these in a minute.

With your Forex trading career, you are now in the position of being both employer and employee. By the time you finish this manual you should be prepared to write up your trading plan. Your trading plan will detail the currency or currencies you plan to trade, the hours you plan to trade, etc. This is the employer side of you; setting forth on paper what is expected of you, the employee. It is your job as the employee to carry out your written plan.

Let's say your trading plan states that you will be trading the London session, and for you this means getting up 2 hours earlier than you are accustomed to set up your charts for the day, plot pivots and study the markets. Will you stay up all night partying and decide to sleep in instead? Will you rush to your charts two hours late and forgo the required preparation time and study? It's your decision of course, because you are totally in charge of your trading career. But if you decide to cut corners and not employ yourself to your optimal level, the paycheck will not be there for you at the end of the week.

Therefore, taking care of your health, keeping a positive mental attitude, eliminating distractions and getting plenty of rest is essential for the trader.

So how do you take care of yourself? Here are a few areas that deserve your attention.

Rest

Trading is fun, but it is also exhausting. Many hours are spent in front of the charts studying and waiting for the high probability set-up. Having a trade set up perfectly or managing a trade to the end might take you to the middle of night. It is essential that you learn to make your rest/sleep a priority so that you are mentally strong and ready for your next session.

Traders who are overtired will be prone to deviating from their trading plan or making impulsive decisions that can gobble up profits.

Plan your rest/sleeping hours as strictly as you plan your trading hours. Trading is a job that requires mental alertness and you want to give yourself every advantage possible. If something has prevented you from getting all the rest you need, or you are over-tired, do not trade.

As you progress in your trading, there are advanced techniques you can use like getting alerts from your broker or setting alarms on your charts so that you can rest while the market is not going your way, and come back to your charts when the set up you have been waiting for is unfolding.

Do not make the mistake of thinking you can trade proficiently without giving your body and your mind the proper rest it requires.

Distractions

Distractions come in all forms. They can be something that is pleasurable; such as watching TV, taking a phone call or visiting with family. They can also be unpleasant; like an unexpected car repair, a cold, or a knock at your door by a salesman. However, trading is an activity that requires your full attention and your job is to eliminate distractions from your trading day.

Make sure that you have set up your trading station in a quiet place. You should plan to focus entirely on your trading. Do not watch TV or even have the radio playing in the background. Do not pay bills or engage in some side activity while trading. Do not talk on the phone while trading. Even a quick phone call can break your concentration. You may return to your charts to see that the market moved significantly while you were chatting.

If your trading station is not in a room that can be closed off from family, make sure that family does not become a distraction. Many family members, including children, may be interested in what you are doing. If they want to be with you while you are working then make sure you incorporate them into the trading plan. You should be teaching anyone in the room with you what you are doing. If you start to explain your charts, pivot points, candle formations, etc. to anyone who is watching, this will benefit in two ways. It will immediately reinforce what you already know and help your learning curve. It will also display to the people around you that trading is a serious business. That what you are doing is work. If they continue to have an interest, great! They might just become a trader too. Then you will have a trading partner and a second set of eyes to help you determine chart patterns, etc. If they are not really interested, they will naturally slip away and your distraction will slip away as well.

Remember, distractions can come in many forms. If you feel like something is nagging you in the back of your mind (a recent car problem, a friend's illness, problems on the job) then stay away from trading until you can come to your charts with a clear head.

Mental Attitude

Many articles have been written that suggest your mental attitude might just be the single most important skill you bring to your trading career. Just like many great athletes over the years have won or lost based not on their skills, but on their mental discipline during the game.

Tiger Woods is a good example of this. Rarely does anyone see him display any emotion during the game because he is so mentally focused. Whether his last shot was a bad one (i.e. a losing trade) or a good one (i.e. a winning trade) he has conditioned himself to keep his mental attitude strong, upbeat and focused on his next shot. You need to do this as well.

If you feel that you are a naturally pessimistic person, this may be a skill that you need to work on more than the next trader. Even if you are a generally positive person, outside events can cause anyone to have a "bad day".

If you are having a bad day for any reason, it is best not to bring those emotions to the marketplace with you. Take a break. Get some exercise. Involve yourself in a hobby you enjoy until your positive mental attitude is restored. Then take that positive attitude to the market and bring home some profits.

Diet/Nutrition/Exercise

Most people overlook how their diet affects all areas of their lives. If you haven't paid attention to it before, now is a good time.

Sure, we have all heard that nutrition is important. Maybe that hasn't been enough to cause you to make better choices on what you put into your body. But what if someone told you that your profits were going to be in direct proportion to what you eat? Would that cause you to take it more seriously?

The reality is that the quality of food we put into our bodies impacts how we are able to perform. This includes the mental performance that is required of us while trading.

If you live on a diet of sugar, caffeine and fat, you will be sluggish; both your body and your mind. Trading requires that you be alert. How can you give yourself the edge you need? By paying attention to what is going in your mouth.

It's not enough to eat a healthy meal, and then bring a cup of coffee and some donuts with you to your trading station. Eating sugary foods will give you a short-term rush, but quickly cause a drop in blood sugar and subsequently a drop in mental focus. You can't afford to lose mental focus in the Forex market. You are trading against thousands of other traders who have prepared themselves mentally and your money is on the line.

Ironic as it may sound, if you trade while you are a little bit hungry, you are actually giving yourself an edge. When we eat, blood is diverted to the stomach to digest the meal. This is blood that is being diverted from your brain! We want as much blood flowing to the brain as possible to give us the mental focus we need for trading.

Plenty of lean protein, vegetables, fruit and fiber will give your body what it needs to perform at an optimum level in all areas of your life.

Need even more of an edge? Then here is some good news for you. In addition to the foods you choose to eat, there are herbs and supplements that have been proven to enhance mental clarity and focus. Ginkgo Biloba, Guarana and Ginseng are just a few. These products can increase the blood flow to the brain without the letdown that sugar and caffeine can cause.

These types of products are readily available to consumers today. Generally speaking, you will get a higher quality product if you find a distributor who will work with you, as opposed to buying them from the local drugstore or supermarket where you are not assured of the quality or the age of the product.

Now that you are eating better and thinking more clearly, you may find you want to get out and move a little more. Exercise! We all need exercise and it's the perfect break from your trading. Push yourself away from your trading station at regular intervals and get some exercise. You'll get the blood pumping to all parts of your body, release endorphins that will boost your mental attitude, and more than likely it will add years to your life!

As a trader you need every edge you can give yourself. Do not forget these seemingly insignificant, but very important aspects of your trading career.

Final Comments

You have now learned two of the most significant trading tools, pivots points and COT data, which the 'Big Dog' traders use to their advantage. Additionally, you have also learned several basic trading indicators used by experienced traders. With this information, you will now have more of an advantage in trading the Forex.

You should consider your initial completion of this course as the beginning of your trading journey, not the end. There is always something you can learn from other traders, whether they are novice or experienced traders.

Please spend the time to learn how your indicators work. Do not jump to every new indicator that you hear about or you will get lost on your journey. Instead, do what seasoned traders do: stay the course and continue to develop your trading skills.

Work and learn at a pace your current lifestyle will allow, do not rush it. The market will always be there. There will always be great trades to come. With patience and persistence, you will steadily gain invaluable experience that will lead to good trading decisions.

Stay focused, work hard, and believe in yourself. Remember, success is determined one trade at a time.

We wish you all the best.

From Peter and the Forexmentor Team

Glossary

- A -

Appreciation – A currency is said to 'appreciate' when it's increasing in price.

Ask Rate - The price at which the currency pair or security is offered for sale, the quoted price at which an investor can buy a currency pair. This is also known as the offer, ask price, and ask rate.

Authorized Dealer – A financial broker, institution or bank authorized to deal in foreign exchange.

- B -

Balance of Trade – The value of exports less imports for a particular country. A trade deficit is when a country imports more than it exports. A trade surplus is when a country exports more than it imports.

Bank of Japan or BOJ – The central bank of Japan.

Base currency – The first currency listed in the in the currency pair. In the GBP/USD pair the GBP would be the base currency.

Bear Market – A market characterized by declining prices.

Bear Trap – The condition in the market where traders who are short an investment product are forced to cover their position because a rising market condition.

Bear - A trader who believes that price is going to decline.

Bid Rate - The price at which a trader is willing to buy currency.

Breakdown – A drop below a level of price support.

Breakout – A rise in a currency's price above a resistance level.

Broker - An individual or firm, who executes orders to buy and sell currencies and related instruments either for a commission or on a spread.
Bull Market - A prolonged period of generally rising prices for a particular investment product.

Bull - A trader who believes that prices will rise.

- C -

Cable - A nickname used in the foreign exchange market for the USD/GBP rate.

Central Bank - A bank, which is responsible for controlling a country's monetary policy. The Federal Reserve is the central bank for the United States, the European Central Bank is the central bank of Europe, the Bank of England is the central bank of England and the Bank of Japan is the central bank of Japan. Traditionally, its primary responsibility is development and implementation of monetary policy.

Central Bank Intervention – The act by which a central bank or central banks enter the spot foreign exchange market and attempt to influence unbalanced supply and demand forces through the direct purchase or sale of foreign exchange.

CFTC - The Commodity Futures Trading Commission, the US Federal regulatory agency for futures traded on commodity markets, including financial futures.

Close – The price of the last transaction of a currency on a particular candle in the respective time frame you are viewing. Technically there is no open or closing of the Forex market.

Commission - The fee paid to a broker or bank for executing a trade based on the number of lots traded.

Commitments of Traders (COT) – A report published every Friday by the Commodity Futures Trading Commission (CFTC) that seeks to provide investors with up-to-date information on futures market operations.

Counter Currency – The second currency in a currency pair. In the currency pair GBP/USD, the counter currency is the USD.

Cross Currency Pair – Rates between two currencies, neither of which is paired with the US Dollar.

Currency – Any form of money issued by a government or central bank and used as a basis for trade.

Currency Pair – The two currencies in a foreign exchange transaction. The EUR/JPY is an example of a currency pair.

- D -

Day Trading – The opening and closing the same position or positions within one trading day.

Dealer - An individual or firm acting as a principal, rather than as an agent, in the purchase and/or sale of foreign exchange. Dealers trade for their own account and risk.

Deficit – A negative balance of trade or payments.

Depreciation - A fall in the value of a currency.

Devaluation – The downward adjustment of a currency against its fixed parities or bands, normally initiated by a formal announcement by a country.

Divergence – When price and indicator fail to stay in sync and move in the opposite direction of each other.

Domestic Rates - The interest rates applicable to deposits in the country of origin.

- E -

Economic Indicator – A government issued statistic that indicates current economic status of the country it reports on. Common indicators include employment rates, inflation, manufacturing sales etc.

EFT – Electronic Fund Transfer.

Exotic - A very thinly traded currency.

- F -

Federal Reserve System - The central banking system of the United States.

Fixed Exchange Rate - Official rate set by monetary authorities. Often the fixed exchange rate permits fluctuation within a band.

Foreign Exchange – The simultaneous buying of one currency and selling of another.

Forex – Term used to describe the foreign exchange market.

Fundamental Analysis – Analysis based on economic statistics and reports.

Fundamentals - The macro economic factors that are accepted as forming the foundation for the relative value of a currency, these include inflation, growth, trade balance, government deficit, and interest rates.

FX – Acronym for the Foreign Exchange market.

- G -

"Good Till Cancelled" (GTC) - An order left with a dealer to buy or sell at a fixed price. It holds until cancelled.

Going long - The act of buying a currency pair. For example, if a client bought the EUR/USD, he would be "going long" the Euro and expecting price action on the chart to go up.

Going short – The act of selling a currency pair. For example, if a client sold the EUR/USD, he would be "going short" the Euro and expecting price action on the chart to go down.

- H -

Hedged Position – One open buy position and one open sell position in the same currency where price movement in either direction offsets any profit or loss.

- I -

IMF - International Monetary Fund.

Inflation – The rate at which the prices for goods and services is rising.

Initial Margin - The deposit required before a client can open a position in the market.

- K -

Kiwi - Slang for the New Zealand dollar.

- L -

Limit Order - An order where the client specifies a price and the order can be executed only if the market reaches that price.

Liquidity – The term used to describe the amount of volume available to buy or sell at a point in time.

Long - The term used to describe a client who has opened a new position by buying the base currency in the pair it is associated with.

- M -

Maintenance Margin - The minimum margin that a trader must keep to maintain an open position.

Margin Call - A demand for additional funds to be deposited in a margin account to meet margin requirements because of adverse exchange rate movements.

Market Order – An immediate order to buy or sell a currency at the time the order is received in the market, at the best possible price.

Moving Average - A way of smoothing a period of price data by taking the sum of the period and dividing it by the length of the period to obtain the average price over time.

- O -

Offer - The price at which a broker or bank is willing to sell the currency. The Offer is also called the Ask.

Overbought – The extremes of price movement to the upside where prices are likely to run out of buying pressures as determined by a technical indicator like stochastic.

Overnight Position – A trade that remains open until the next business day.

Oversold – The extremes of price movement to the downside where prices are likely to run out of selling pressure as determined by a technical indicator like stochastic.

- P -

Pip – The smallest unit of price for any foreign currency.

- R -

Rally – A large move in price - either up or down.

Resistance Level – Price level where selling pressures are strong enough to prevent price from continuing to advance.

Retracement – When price pull back against its current rally, whether that rally be up or down.

Rollover – At the end of each business day, the broker or bank will automatically rollover or swap, all existing open positions into the next spot date. The cost of this process is based on the interest rate differential of the two currencies.

- S -

Short – Having an open position that was created by selling a currency. If you sold the AUD/USD, the client is said to be "Short" the currency pair (sold the base currency). If a client bought the AUD/USD, he would be long the currency pair, but short USD currency. Foreign exchange transactions assume being long one currency and short another due to the fact it is a simultaneous transaction.

Short Covering - Buying to close a short position.

Spot - Spot or Spot date refers to the spot transaction value date that is two business days, subject to value date calculation. In instances where there is holiday, weekend or other day when the banks in the countries represented by the currencies in the currency pair are closed, the spot date will be adjusted forward to the next value date where the banks are open.

Spot Price/Rate - The price at which a currency pair is currently trading in the spot market.

Spread - The difference between the bid and ask prices.

Sterling – Slang for British pound, otherwise known as cable.

Stop-loss order – A specific order entered by the trader to close out a position if the price moves in the opposite direction the trader anticipated the position to move by a certain amount of pips.

Support Level – Price level where buying pressure is stronger than the selling pressure. Support levels prevent price from further decline.

Swissy - Market slang for Swiss Franc.

- T -

Technical Analysis - Analysis based on price action through chart study and technical indicators.

Thin Trading – A market in which trading volume is low and bid and ask quotes are wide.

Trading Range – The difference between the high and low prices traded during a period of time.

Transaction date - The date on which a trade occurs.

- U -

U.S. Prime Rate – The interest rate at which U.S. banks will lend to their prime corporate customers.

- V -

Volatility - A measure of price fluctuation.

- W -

Whipsaw – A description of a highly volatile market where a sharp price movement is quickly followed by a sharp reversal.

Index

1

1-2-3 Bottoms 34, 37
1-2-3 Tops 34, 35

A

Average Daily Range 136

B

bear flag 47
bull flag 46

C

Calculating Pivot Points 61, 68
Candlesticks 78, 79, 80, 92
CFTC 152, 155, 247
Choosing a broker 208
Commitment of Traders 155, 157, 158
common sense trendline 99, 100, 101, 103, 108, 110
consolidating 22, 23
COT 152, 154, 157, 158, 244, 247
Currency Pairs 193, 194

D

demand trendline 109, 110
demo account 208, 230, 234, 236
demo trading 208, 231
divergence 117, 118, 122, 123, 125, 126, 170, 171, 175, 247
doji 80, 81, 82, 83, 84, 88
double bottom 34, 40, 42
double top 34, 39, 42, 175

H

hammer 87, 88, 89, 90, 175
head and shoulders 34, 43, 44, 45, 136, 140, 141, 166
Head and Shoulders Price Projection 136, 140, 141
histogram 117, 118, 119, 120

I

inverted head and shoulders 34, 45, 140, 141, 166

L

Limit Entry Order 215
Limit Order 215, 249

M

M1/M3 .... 72, 73, 171, 175
M2/M4 .... 72, 73, 89, 175
MACD 116, 117, 118, 119, 120, 122, 123, 125, 126, 166, 168, 169, 170, 171, 175, 225, 226
Market Order 214, 249

N

Negative Divergence 123
neutralization 122, 125, 126, 175
news 26, 144, 145, 198, 200, 201, 209

P

patience 186, 187, 198
Pennants 34, 49
pip 172, 194, 195, 250
pivot points 56, 58, 59, 60, 61, 62, 66, 71, 72, 74, 98, 170, 175, 239, 244
Positive Divergence 123
price projections 136, 175

R

railroad tracks 93, 94, 171
rallying 22, 23
real money 116, 208, 234, 236
resistance 26, 27, 28, 29, 30, 56, 58, 59, 98, 99, 108, 110, 164, 165, 167, 246, 250
risk management 180

S

spinning tops 84, 85, 86, 175
stochastics 130, 131, 132, 133, 166, 168, 169, 170, 171, 227, 228
Stop Order 216
supply trendline 107, 108, 110
support 26, 28, 29, 30, 56, 58, 59, 71, 98, 99, 108, 110, 164, 165, 167, 169, 171, 246, 250
swing high 105, 107, 108, 109, 110
swing low 106, 107, 109, 110

T

Taking Care of the Trader 238

Term	Pages
Time of Day	145, 146, 147, 148
Tom DeMark Trendlines	104, 108, 110
top down trading	164, 173, 175
trading plan	61, 204, 205, 238, 239
trendline	94, 98, 99, 100, 102, 104, 108, 110, 166, 167, 169, 171
Triangle Price Projection	136, 138, 139
triangles	34, 50, 52, 138
Triple Bottoms	34, 42
Triple Tops	34, 42

Made in the USA